THE HEROIC PATH

"Let the heroic path lead you to an understanding of curing and healing. What is true good health? What is the meaning of life? Who are you as an individual, and how would you introduce yourself to God? I think this book will help you find the answers to these questions."

—Bernie S. Siegel, M.D., author of
Love, Medicine and Miracles and *Peace, Love and Healing*

"Angela is a woman of authenticity and love, a woman to listen to. She gives wisdom and clarity and lives what she says. She's a real power of example of a healthy, conscious human being."

—Dr. Susan Cooley Ricketson,
psychotherapist, author of *The Dilemma of Love:
Healing Co-dependent Relationships at Different Stages of Life*

"My time with Angela has been revolutionary. I highly recommend her for anyone stuck on the spiritual path of recovery. She'll make you laugh, cry, look at yourself and, most of all, help you find your way in life."

—Christopher Hebard

"Angela's gift for seeing into people astounds me! She is nothing short of a miracle on earth. I have the deepest love and the greatest respect for who she is and what she does."

—R. Pavilionis

"I am convinced that Angela will become the most important holistic healer in America. Her commitment to her work is total. Her ability to articulate emotionally to people with terminal or critical illness is profound."

—David Hoffman, Varied Directions International

THE HEROIC PATH

One Woman's Journey
from Cancer to Self-Healing

How to heal yourself
of life-threatening illness,
find your true self, and make life work!

Angela Passidomo Trafford

Blue Dolphin Publishing
1993

Published by Blue Dolphin Publishing, Inc.
P.O. Box 1908, Nevada City, California 95959

ISBN: 0-931892-55-4

Library of Congress Cataloging in Publication Data

Trafford, Angela Passidomo
    The heroic path : one woman's journey from cancer to
self-healing / Angela Passidomo Trafford
        p.   cm.
    Includes bibliographical references.
    ISBN 0-931892-55-4 : $12.95
    1. Trafford, Angela Passidomo—Health.   2. Breast—
Cancer—Patients—United States—Biography.
    3. Visualization.   4. Healing.
    RC280.B8T72 1993
    362.1'9699449'0092—dc20
        [B]   93-10894
                                                                  CIP

Cover art: Maxfield Parrish (1870-1966), Ecstasy, 1929.

Printed in the United States of America by
Blue Dolphin Press, Inc., Grass Valley, California

9   8   7   6   5   4   3   2   1

Dedication

- To God, the Creator, I bow in humble gratitude to your divine ever-present grace, guidance, protection and love.

- To "The Man in Black."

- To my children, John, Richard and Michael—young hero warriors, travellers on the Heroic Path—thank you for *your* unconditional love, boundless joy, and for never losing faith in me.

- To Bernie Siegel—Soul connection, words cannot express my gratitude. Thank you for believing in me.

- To my parents, Rose and Don Passidomo, thank you for having me.

- To Carol Jean Brooks—my dearest friend, thank you for being there for me.

- To my many clients at Self-Healing—thank you for all your courage and faith—you are all my teachers.

- To all the children of this earth who cry for unconditional love—this book is my gift to you.

- Thank you, Mother Earth, for your beauty and magnificence, for your loving, delightful, innocent creatures, my teachers and protectors, who took me home and healed my sorrow. There are no words to express the unspeakable joy.

- To Father Sky—thank you for revealing to me the Great Secret.

Acknowledgments

- To Joyce Boaz—thank you for your belief in me and my work, and your tireless efforts on my behalf.

- To Helen Foley, who helps me from the other side.

- To Jo Ann Smallwood, Russell Rosen, Ted Norris, Carl Todd—thank you for your love and support.

- To René—thank you for awakening part of me.

- To Paul Clemens for your patience and wisdom, and Corinn Codye for your marvelous ideas and editorial skills—thank you both for helping me give birth to this book.

To be or not to be—
That is the question.
Whether 'tis nobler in the mind
To bear the slings and arrows
Of outrageous fortune—
Or to take arms
Against a sea of troubles
And by opposing them
End them

—William Shakespeare, *Hamlet*

૪

We have not even to risk the adventure alone,
For the heroes of all time have gone before us.
The labyrinth is thoroughly known.

We have only to follow the thread of the hero's path
And where we had thought to find an abomination,
We shall find a God.
And where we had thought to slay another,
We shall slay ourselves.

Where we had thought to travel outward,
We shall come to the center of our own existence.

Where we had thought to be alone,
We shall be with all the world.

—Joseph Campbell

And a woman spoke, saying, Tell us of Pain.

And he said:

Your pain is the breaking of the shell that encloses your understanding.

Even as the stone of the fruit must break, that its heart may stand in the sun, so must you know pain.

And could you keep your heart in wonder at the daily miracles of your life, pain would not seem less wondrous than your joy, even as you have always accepted the seasons that pass over your fields.

And you would watch with serenity through the winters of your grief.

Much of your pain is self-chosen.

It is the bitter potion by which the physician within you heals your sick self.

Therefore trust the physician, and drink his remedy in silence and tranquility:

For his hand, though heavy and hard, is guided by the tender hand of the Unseen,

And the cup he brings, though it burn your lips, has been fashioned of the clay which the Potter has moistened with His own sacred tears.

—Kahlil Gibran, *The Prophet*

Contents

Foreword

It is important for us to realize that it is a heroic journey to search for the gift in an affliction or adverse circumstance. However, charcoal does not become a diamond unless it is exposed to pressure. I do not think it is appropriate for anyone to tell another person there is a gift in cancer or AIDS. It is only when the individual is ready and willing to undertake the healing journey that he will reveal for himself the treasure hidden in the darkness.

Angela's book can help guide you on that journey. It can help you find your unique path. The ability of a riderless horse to find its way home has taught me a lot.

Angela discusses her path and the dream of a white horse. The symbolism of the riderless horse, or the rider letting go of the reins, appears in many myths and fairy tales. The image is telling us to let go of an intellect constantly tugging on the reins and deciding where we are to go. It is for the hero to let his intuitive knowledge guide him and direct him. It takes courage to let go and respond to this inner knowledge.

When Angela discusses my role in her life you must understand I didn't do anything *for* her. I may have been a guide or teacher, but she responded to my words because of her own resources and desires. She heard what she thought I said. I am given credit for things because of what she did. Other people hear or read the same words and don't respond. So the metaphors applied to me belong to the person using them. Anyone saying I inspired them is an inspiring person.

When I read Angela's book, I am inspired. I learn and relearn from her and her work. This book is a wonderful lesson for me. I can laugh, cry and respond with a "yes" to it all.

As you read this book, please do not let guilt become a problem. We are talking about taking a Heroic Path; that is the victory. Every disease can't be cured and everyone dies, but not everyone lives. This path will teach you to live. Don't let the guilt, fault, blame and shame placed on you by parents, teachers and religions stop you from giving birth to yourself. You are the laboring parent and the newborn, all at the same time.

Let love into your life. Let God, our Creator, into your life. If one of those words bothers you, use the other. They represent the same healing energy available to all of us.

Return to nature and learn from it too. Observe nature and learn how to heal and love under all kinds of adverse situations. You will learn to create your own weather.

Just as nature responds to adversity, you will learn how important our pain is, to awaken us and protect us. We need our physical and emotional pain or we would constantly be subjecting ourselves to injury and further loss.

Ultimately let the heroic path lead you to an understanding of curing and healing. What is true good health? What is the meaning of life? Who are you as an individual, and how would you introduce yourself to God?

I think this book will help you find the answers to these questions. For me health is a state of mind. My life achieves meaning through my way of choosing to love the world, and God knows me. None of us really need an introduction to God.

I hope when you finish this book, you will achieve a healthy life full of meaning and not just play a role, because God doesn't meet with the people who define themselves by labels or the roles they play. God only meets with co-creators.

This book can *help you* find the heroic path to creativity.

Bernie S. Siegel, M.D.

Preface

A few weeks ago, I was cleaning out my closet when I came across an old pocketbook that was filled with paraphernalia from the past.

As I explored the bits and pieces of my life at that time, I realized that this pocketbook was used during my first bout with cancer, nine years ago.

I opened my wallet and explored the contents. I inhaled sharply as I drew out a religious card of St. Jude and remembered St. Jude—patron saint of hopeless causes.

A wave of painful memories flooded through me as I remembered my battle at that time—all the suffering, the falling and picking myself up again, the first panic-filled steps out of a life of sadness, suffering and illness into one of hope, and the first shaky belief in myself.

As I emptied the contents of the wallet, I found, secretly wedged underneath a leather flap, a weathered, folded piece of paper that was tearing into pieces at the fold lines, so often had it been opened, read, and refolded.

With great, great care I gently unfolded it and read the faded, pencilled words . . .

Oh! Those feelings came back as I remembered the words I had written to give myself courage and support as I made the decision to leave my painful marriage, despite being financially busted and having a lump in my breast that was diagnosed as cancer.

My eyes filled with tears of joy and compassion as I read the prophetic words, written by another me in another life so long ago. It is a quote from Colette, the free-spirited French authoress.

"No, I do not shudder. All that is life, time flowing on,
The hoped for miracle that may lie round
The next bend of the road . . ."

and then, underlined:

"It is because of my faith in that miracle that I am escaping."

Introduction

Cancer was the best thing that ever happened to me. It totally changed my life. Let me amend that: I allowed it to totally change my life. I allowed it to enter my life like the spirit of truth and crack me down, crack down my resistance to change—my hardened, unforgiving ways, the fear that ruled my actions and thoughts, the hopelessness and negativity that ruled my being and, worst of all, my determination to have my own way and be proven RIGHT, even though the tragedy and pain of my existence showed otherwise.

Cancer was the last straw in the battleground between my inner self and my outer world, in the out-of-control existence that was my life for so many years.

Cancer entered my world as a harbinger of truth, light, and love—the unconditional love so lacking in myself since childhood. All that sadness and anger was stored up in my body and the doctors gave it a name: cancer.

From my standpoint now, I see that God wants each one of us to have a wonderful life. Truly, it is our divine birthright to live a joyful, healthy life. The problem each one of us faces is how to do that.

Well, there is a way to do it, for those of you with the courage, spirit and will power to get on your path in life and go forward out of fear, into finding out what it truly means to unconditionally love yourself and others. Cancer, when handled properly, can put you on your path in life. My own life is testimony to the absolute fact that with the help of God you can change your life from tragedy and adversity, as I have, to love, joy, inner peace and health.

What I really want to do in this book is, first, inspire you that this is possible and, second, give you the guidance and tools to take on the challenge of the illness of cancer and use it to transform your life. You can do this—all of you out there with the courage to change. This book is for all the heroes, those with illness, or those fortunate enough to realize the need to change your lives from anger, sadness, fear and confusion, into health and life.

You can do it!

I am now on the heroic path, and if I can live this way, any one of you can. If you can say that life is indeed a mystery, that there is more for you to learn, if you are seeking answers, then don the robes of the hero and read on.

I have had the honor and privilege of working with many heroes in the course of this work—people who have had the courage to step forward out of fear and to allow cancer to become a vehicle for the transformation and empowerment of their lives. All these truly courageous and wonderful people have been teachers to me of the highest order, for through their tremendous sharing and communication, the agony and ecstasy of change, the unlocking of painful childhood memories, and the releasing of pain from the past, these heroes have taught me about life and how to live life. I would like to share with you their amazing, moving stories, information I have learned from having the privilege to have worked on an intimate basis with my fellow human beings and, from having had the privilege of experiencing the supreme adventure of healing and rebirth, the cancer journey.

This book is for you, all the heroes.

1

Let us choose love and life.

—Last line in *Love, Medicine and Miracles*
by Dr. Bernie Siegel

Coincidence is God's way of remaining anonymous.

—Dr. Bernie Siegel

Often, the test of courage is not to die, but to live.

—Vittorio Alfieri Oreste

My Story: I Choose Life

I had cancer twice. The first time, eight years ago, it appeared
as a lump in my right breast. I denied the presence of that lump
for eleven months, until I finally saw a doctor. The denial was
totally in accord with my life at that time, a life lived denying
my true feelings and well being. When the doctor told me I had
cancer, I cried uncontrollably for hours. I crash-landed into the
reality of my feelings, the reality of my life. At that time, I lived
up in Canada, in a log cabin in the woods. I was in an unhappy,
abusive marriage, in an isolated, sterile existence. Even without
having any information or books about this illness available to
me at that time, I instinctively knew what this disease was all
about; I knew it meant I needed to change my life or die.

I chose life. I divorced my husband and came to grips with
the pain of my life. I had no idea how I would survive; I couldn't
figure it out. I only knew the time was **now** to change; there was
no time to waste. My first step towards self-esteem happened in
the hospital, as I stood up to my doctor and determined for

myself the course of treatment that felt right for me. I opted for a lumpectomy, which went against the mastectomy the surgeon wanted to perform. I don't recommend this course of action for everyone; I just knew it was right for me. I knew it was right because I began at that time to go inside myself and honor my feelings. As painful as it was, I began making decisions that felt right for me. I took charge of my illness and my life. I then went through eight months of chemotherapy and radiation treatments. At this time, I began to realize that, in accordance with taking charge of my health and happiness, life seemed to come to my support in many miraculous ways that I could not foresee or expect. In the midst of all these painful decisions, while raising by myself a baby and two small boys, I met a man who fell passionately in love with me and—truly through his help, love and attention—aroused renewed inspiration within myself to not only survive, but to live. I remarried and moved to Florida.

My health improved, my hair grew back and my life changed. Then a tragedy occurred. My ex-husband kidnaped my children and brought them back to Canada. Years of suffering and three custody trials later, I lost the custody of my beloved three boys. Within ten minutes on the same morning, I received two phone calls. The first call said that I had lost the custody of my children. The second call was from my doctor, saying that I had a recurrence of cancer. I cannot convey to you the suffering I felt at that time. My children were my life; I could not conceive of going on without them. Furthermore, I had no money and no way of even seeing them again. I saw no reason for a future. I considered suicide. I was in so much pain that I could no longer stand to be inside my own body.

This was the final blow to me, the "blow that none could parry." I remember at that time raging against God at what I considered the total unfairness and tragedy of my life. I realized my consideration of suicide was another attempt to manipulate God to my own ends. I realized in that moment of truth that I could not manipulate God. My ego admitted defeat.

I got down on my knees in my living room at that moment and admitted that I wanted to live. I had this tremendous realization that I had never understood that the gift of life itself was an extraordinarily miraculous fact in and of itself; I realized also that I had never wanted to embrace life for myself—it was always for someone else. I had somehow lost my way in life and needed to find my path. I humbled myself and asked God for help.

I admitted that I did not know how to live, that all my attempts at living life had ended in tragedy, pain and illness. I let go of my life to God and asked God to show me how to live.

Without knowing exactly where I was going or why, I got into my car and began to aimlessly drive in a haze of fear and suffering. Fully alive to the realities of my life for perhaps the first time, I spotted the sign of a fortune teller and turned into the driveway. When this woman answered the door, upon one look at my face she said, "I don't know what has happened to you, but this will all turn around for you in the next few years." I hung onto these words for dear life.

I then found myself wandering through the public library. I will never forget this moment. The librarian, whom I did not know, came up to me with a book in her hands. I stared at the title. It was Dr. Bernie Siegel's *Love, Medicine and Miracles*. She said, "Have you read this book?" When I shook my head no, she promptly replied, "Well, you should!"

I took the book home and cried as I read it. Here within these pages were all the answers for which I had been searching. I knew this was the answer to my prayer. I wept tears of gratitude, thanking God for this great gift. The humility and gratitude were a welcome relief, a balm to my soul. It was a joy to look to God for help instead of having to bluff my way through life, pretending to know it all. I asked God to forgive me for the way I had been living, to take my life and show me the way.

In the next few weeks, with the help of God, I began to take charge of my life and my health. I used the three weeks before my scheduled surgical biopsy to once again change my life and take on the responsibility for my health and happiness.

I began rising at dawn and watching the first pink rays of sunlight sweeping the sky. I reached inside and thanked God for each new day, releasing tears of gratitude, which were followed by an immense rush of energy that was none other than the healing energy of hope. I would then take a ride on my bicycle, fully alive in the moment, feeling like a child again. After my bike ride, I would return home, sit on the couch in front of my aquarium, and begin the meditation and visualization exercises outlined in Bernie's book.

To my amazement, a visualization came forth from within myself of little birds eating golden crumbs; the little birds were the immune system cells and the golden crumbs the cancer cells. It was truly amazing to me that I visualized the cancer in that form of golden crumbs, buttery and rich. I would follow this visualization by imagining a white light coming through the top of my head, flowing through my body, healing me.

After almost three weeks, one morning, after returning from my bike ride, I sat down on my couch to meditate. As I began my visualization of the little birds, all of a sudden, unsolicited by myself, I felt the white light flow through the top of my head with tremendous energy and force. I remember the exact experience—it was the experience of my duality as a human being. As this tremendous heat, this energy was flowing through my body, my heart was pounding violently. My rational mind, the ego, in all its customary fear, was shouting, "Get up! Get up! You're having a heart attack! Stop the experience!" I remember a calm, detached awareness at that moment—that my intellectual mind was nothing but a tape, a relentless tape recording of fear and mistrust. I did not think of anything at all at that moment, but simply let go to the experience. I chose to let go and allow my being to become one with that beautiful light, that powerful energy.

Afterward, I slumped over on the couch. For the first time in my life, my mind was free of all thought. For the first time in my life, I experienced a deep, silent peace, like a smile in my heart. I knew something wonderful had happened. When my husband returned home, I said, "I wish they would take another mammogram. I'll bet they won't find anything there."

I told my family about my experience. They looked at me with skepticism and said nothing.

Later on that week, I went for another mammogram. The doctor came into the room and put up all the previous x-rays for me to see, showing me the cancerous dark shadow. Afterward he left the room, and I undressed for the mammogram. I was in a state of balance inside myself, not fearful, just curious and aware. It was as if someone inside myself, an intelligence, was watching the movie of my life. This intelligence, this awareness, had all the answers and was aware of the outcome.

After the technician took the mammogram, I got dressed again and was waiting for the doctor when the technician poked her head in the door, smiling, saying, "The doctor wants just one more mammogram."

I undressed for another mammogram. This happened eight times!

At the end of the eighth time, the doctor came bounding into the room and told me what I already knew—that the cancer had disappeared. He was very excited and happy for me, but mystified. I told him about the little birds and the golden crumbs, about the white light. He looked into my eyes, took both my hands in his, and said with true sincerity, "Call it little birds, or call it what you will, but you are a very lucky woman."

I shared the wonderful news with my mother and family. They were all so happy for me, happy and amazed. There was a hushed silence and a wonderful light in everybody's eyes. It was a miracle.

I allowed this experience to totally change my life. I began to feel a purpose, a mission in life to share my experience with others facing the illness of cancer. I began to volunteer my services in the cancer ward at the hospital, filling water jugs and sharing my experience with the seriously ill.

It took a lot of courage to do this, but I was now in touch with an inner voice, a gentle, loving, inner voice that was a guiding force in my life. I saw and felt such hopelessness and resignation within the cancer ward, not only in the patients, but in the doctors and nursing staff as well. I began to realize, as Dr. Carl Simonton asserts, that cancer was indeed a disease of hopelessness. I began to realize through my own experience, and through communicating deeply and honestly with the people in the hospital, that the roots of cancer were emotional, deeply imbedded in pain and inner suffering, and that the first step to wellness was a feeling of hope that healing was possible.

Some people, deeply into the drama of their lives as I had been, turned their backs on my message of hope. I saw that these people were entrenched in their patterns of hopelessness and despair and had already chosen to die; others were too fearful and timid to allow hope of change.

But there were so many who took my message to heart with joy and hope, sharing their stories with me with gratitude and hope for change. I began to sense a need in people to share and commune on a deep level, and that this sharing and under-standing could change people's lives and health.

I saw courageous people die within days of being told by their doctor that there was no hope for them. I saw that human beings with cancer needed help, encouragement, vision and guidance to survive.

I tried to institute a program within the hospital, a program of therapy, meditation and visualization, which I saw to be every bit as important as medical treatment and medicine.

When bureaucratic red tape prevented me from instituting my program at the hospital, I went out on a limb about five miles long and opened up my own practice, Self-Healing. It was the realization of a dream for me and it was scary. I wrote to that courageous, brilliant maverick, Dr. Bernie Siegel, and told him of my experience. As usual his startling reply was not what I expected. "Organizations stifle," he wrote. "This way you will grow."

You know, that really blew me away. It really moved me, got to me, that this wonderful, eminent man had taken the time and energy to write back to me. That was the start of another miracle for me, a relationship with a dynamic humanitarian, a brilliant mind, a wonderful soul, who truly devotes his life to helping others empower themselves and change their lives towards peace, love and healing.

How right you were, Bernie Siegel. I planted those words of support in my inner garden and now the lush blossoms are flowering and the fruit is ripening on the tree.

Bernie Siegel is a hero. The first time I met Bernie was when I invited him down to speak and conduct a workshop in Naples, Florida. Bernie actually emanated a white light of power and energy, and I was totally in awe of him. When I picked him and Bobbie, his wife, up at the hotel, I was driving a car I had borrowed from my girlfriend because my own battered Firebird was over the hill and not fit for the likes of the famous Dr. Siegel. The only problem was that my girlfriend's car had a standard shift and I really didn't know how to use it. Undaunted by this minor inconvenience, I fearlessly drove my chariot to the hotel to receive Bernie and Bobbie.

As we entered the vehicle, Bernie calmly informed me that he was on a mission from God. This really got my attention. I had waited years to meet him and talk with him and I couldn't get enough.

As we sailed through red lights, gears grinding away, Bernie sat calmly cracking jokes in the back seat. I thought his jokes were hilarious and my body responded by stepping hard on the brake pedal when I laughed, so we would all go flying forward in the car.

When we arrived at the church, which was mobbed, I couldn't get the windows down to inform the guard that I had the honored speaker with me and needed a personal escort to the front of the church. I couldn't stop the car either, so we sailed through a line of crossing guards who quickly scattered to save their lives while Bernie shouted in vain against the closed window, "I'm the speaker!" He'll do anything to get attention.

It was great! It was like being with a childhood buddy, except it was my beloved mentor, the renowned Dr. Bernie Siegel.

People cringe in fear of Bernie because he is so brilliant, so learned, so powerfully on the mark—a laser beam of intelligence. But to me, he radiates love. He gave me that unconditional love I so needed and that love has meant everything to me.

How many people do you know who freely give of themselves? Who give love? Well, this tells you a little bit of what Bernie Siegel is all about. I'm sure there are thousands of people who could relate stories about how Bernie has affected their lives. He really is becoming a legend in his own time. But, you know, none of those stories would be like mine, because I have a special connection. Somehow I can see him for who he is. He is an especially humble man who cares a great deal. He is real and unique. It's great to be near him. There's simply not enough of Bernie to go around.

Few people know that not only is Bernie a surgeon, healer and speaker, he is also a top-notch artist. His paintings could hang in a museum. He has a tremendous love for human beings, even though he admits, as Martin Luther King has said, "You can't *like* everyone."

Years ago when Bernie was a practicing surgeon, he became despondent about the disease of cancer. Everywhere he looked, it was there. People were dying and there wasn't very much he could do about it. He began to feel hopeless in his ability to help those with cancer. But Bernie didn't lay down and die. He determined to find a way.

He found himself attending a workshop of Dr. Carl Simonton's, where he had strong doubts about the information he was receiving. Meditation? Visualization? Inner work? What was he doing *here* anyway?

Then Bernie had a spiritual experience. He got in touch with his inner guide, George. He shaved his head so he could better receive the light and energy of the Universe. Since then, he hasn't looked back

The excellence of his purpose has blazed a path for him as a true revolutionary hero of the medical profession. Now, our society and attitudes have changed in regard to our perspective regarding illness. Our deeper feelings and attitudes are respected and valued. The whole human being is acknowledged as valuable. Much of this is due to Bernie's work. He has empowered us as individuals and as a society. Thanks, Bernie! You're a living example of how a revolution of consciousness inside one individual has the power to uplift the consciousness of the world. Bravo and God bless you.

In being authentic himself, and capable of unconditional love, Bernie gave me permission to be real. It was such a relief! Thank you, Bernie, you were right. **Love does heal.**

A few months ago, I had the privilege of doing a workshop with him, a workshop called, "The Art of Living." That is truly what this work is all about: how to change your perspective on life, challenge your inner beliefs and fears, and get on your path in life. In taking on the challenge and responsibility for your life and using what I call "the gift of cancer" as a vehicle for change, you too can have a wonderful life, a life that we all deserve but often feel too guilty and fearful to embrace.

This book is about how to become real. It is about how to live an authentic life as an authentic human being—what that means and how to *do* it. As you open this book, I hope you are looking for answers, because you will find them. This book is for the seekers of reality, the heroes of tomorrow, looking for the way, today.

2

Resolve to be thyself; and know that
he who finds himself, loses his misery.

—MATTHEW ARNOLD, *Self-Dependence*

To realize Love is to realize God. If we sit before an
open fire, it warms us. There is no effort on our part.
Those who have realized God are like this fire.
Keep in their company.

—Sufi master, *Daughter of Fire*

I celebrate myself, and sing myself.

—WALT WHITMAN, *Song of Myself*

The Kingdom of God is within you.

Bible, Luke 17:21

What Does It Mean to Love Yourself?—Finding Unconditional Love

Many people suffer from a crippling illness: lack of self-esteem. We harbor inward fantasies and dreams of what we would like our lives to be, but many of us have lost the creative vision and belief in ourselves that would allow us to empower that cherished dream. I saw a bumper sticker the other day which said, "Now that I've given up hope, I feel much better."

Many people secretly feel this sense of despair. In giving away our power to others, we have lost control of our lives.

Women in particular make the mistake of looking to build their self-esteem through the men in their lives. They look toward their husbands, boyfriends or lovers for fulfillment and prosperity, forsaking themselves and the responsibility for their lives in the process. Men often respond to this complete devotion with boredom and lose interest in their partner. Someone else comes along sparkling with happiness and life, and how soon and suddenly the devoted partner is left with a sense of rage, failure and wasted years. Many mothers today, frustrated in their relationships with their spouses or abandoned through divorce, then displace the responsibility for their lives on their sons, crippling these children, who then feel too guilty to move forward in life or to form healthy relationships with women.

Being raised in an Italian family, I was taught to take care of my brothers and my father. I was given the message that men were "poor things" who could not take care of themselves. It was a hard job, but somebody had to do it. I spent many of the crucial years of my life trying to rescue flawed, dishonest men from their own selves. I suffered physical and emotional abuse at the hands of my first husband, but somehow felt it my responsibility to heal him. If I could unconditionally love him, I believed he would ultimately change, protect me and fulfill me. His eyes would be filled with gratitude for my enormous sacrifice. Somehow, someday, he would see the light. What nonsense! This belief almost cost me my life. Cancer showed me that I had to find out what it meant to love *myself* unconditionally; only then could I truly love anyone else. However, if you had told me this at the time, I would have denied it and been utterly mystified.

Many women today suffer the same plight. They are barely surviving in relationships with autocratic, egocentric men who are still yoked and tied to controlling mothers, fearful of abandonment.

I truly feel that it is up to women today to take responsibility for their own lives first and foremost. I have learned through harsh life experience that we can only teach others through example. If you are forsaking your own needs for your son or husband, you are not doing anything for anybody; you are only courting disaster and ill health. The demands in such relationships and the expectations we have toward those we are supposedly "helping," are enough to create a demonic bondage that enmeshes us in fear, hatred, jealousy, possessiveness and, ultimately, self-loathing.

When you learn how to love yourself, when you truly feel the right to focus on your needs and become a balanced human being, then you become a light unto yourself and those you love. Only in this manner can we help anybody else. If, as a wife and mother, you reflect responsibility towards yourself and a healthy self-esteem, no one can ever cause you to take any action that would place harm upon yourself; no one can push you or force you to do anything to destroy the happiness of your world. From this perspective, you need not fear getting lost within your marriage relationship. Your mate is then forced to take on the responsibility for his own self in order to respond within the relationship. Only two healthy human beings who stand side by side, yet together, can truly form a loving, healthy relationship. Further, relationship itself means "to respond." Have you ever felt alone in your relationship? Living with a stone wall? Feel that you are never heard? Or, if you have been living with an alcoholic, that your feelings are always diverted and denied?

It is time then to let go and detach from that person and to focus on yourself. Recently I was asked at one of my workshops, "When you love somebody, but know the relationship is destructive, when do you know that it is time to leave the relationship?"

I asked the questioner if she had manifested a health problem. She replied that she had ovarian cancer. "The message is clear," I responded. "The time is now."

Don't wait until you have a health problem like cancer to end a destructive relationship. I'd like to put up a sign in my office, "Relationships Can Kill." They also can heal. If you are miserable or unhappy in a relationship, give yourself the love you need and reach out for help if necessary.

A few months back, at the Art of Living workshop with Bernie Siegel, I was with Bernie and Bobbie as they were registering at the hotel. "Can I help you?" asked the registration clerk. "Are you a therapist?" Bernie replied. Taken aback, the clerk responded, "No." "Then you can't help me," Bernie replied. When I told this anecdote at the workshop, everybody laughed. The point is, we can all improve our lives. Don't be ashamed to reach out for help. Search for a competent person with a solid reputation who can give you the information and support you need. This is loving yourself.

"As I Love and Support Myself, So Does God and the Universe Support Me."

This is the most significant and powerful affirmation I have discovered. What does it mean?

So many times in the course of my life, I have felt sad, angry, or depressed. Sometimes this negativity was so strong that I just couldn't shake it. No matter how I tried not to have the negative feelings, somehow, something within myself just would not budge and break free. Have you ever felt this way?

One day, in desperation, I picked up a mirror and had the courage to look into it, right into my own eyes. I saw the pain and misery in my expression and began to lecture myself, "Come on, now, Angela, you can shake this feeling—come out of it and be happy!" But the pain and misery remained deep within my eyes.

Suddenly, I had an awareness: at a time like this, I did not need a lecture. I instantly knew exactly what it was I needed. It was then that I discovered the Magic Key.

A feeling of relief flooded my being as I looked into my eyes and stated honestly what it was I was feeling. I said, "I don't like the way you feel right now . . . but **I love you and I accept you, just the way you are, and I am taking care of you!"**

I felt the sadness come up and pass through me like a wave. I took a deep breath and let it out. A few minutes later I noticed that I was feeling lighter, happier. The sadness was released through the healing power of love.

This was a tremendous lesson for me. It taught me that the only power that heals is love. Only through loving ourselves and accepting ourselves as we are, can we release the sadness and pain, make room for the joy and grow.

I have used this Magic Key countless times and the transforming effect is truly amazing. Such is the tremendous healing power of love. It is the only thing that works.

When you are feeling unhappy or out of sorts, give yourself the same time and attention you would a beloved child who is feeling hurt or upset. The little child within us is sensitive and responds to love. Criticism just makes us shrivel and die inside. With over ninety-eight percent of our population being raised in dysfunctional homes with adults in charge who have never learned how to love unconditionally, who, then, will give you the unconditional love and total acceptance you need for health and happiness?

It is up to *you* to find that love within yourself. This is what my affirmation means:

As You Love and Support Yourself,
So Does God and the Universe Support You.

It means that unconditional love has to begin inside you, right now. Only then does life raise you up in strange, unexpected ways and fill your life with miracles.

Make a commitment to yourself to love yourself and find joy in your life.

Most people shiver at the thought of commitment, not only to another, but to their own selves! Isn't this amazing? We unconsciously reject our personal happiness in the process, because we are afraid to take on the responsibility for ourselves and our lives.

The reason is that we all fear failure. Because we have been hurt and criticized as children, we no longer believe in ourselves. The feeling of commitment brings on tremendous pain and fear. In our present society, this has become almost commonplace, such is the sorrow within ourselves. Deep within, we feel that we are faulty and defective human beings, unsalvageable and unlovable. If you can identify with this feeling, as I have in my past, please do not allow it to hold you back. Sometimes the pain within seems insurmountable. I can assure you that if you make the commitment to get on your path in life and succeed, that you will, as Thoreau said, "Meet with a success undreamed of in the common hour." Little affirmations and miracles will light your way and helping hands will extend themselves to you, all because it is YOU who lit the candle in the darkness! Being on your path in life is like having a beloved mate who is always there for you, aware of you. It is as if God is winking at you, cheering you on, all because you had the courage to take the first step forward out of fear, into the light.

All my life, I waited for a hero to come into my life riding a beautiful white horse who would rescue me from all the pain of my life and carry me away. With this person, I would always feel safe, because he was there. Well, I never did find that person. So I took on the responsibility for my life and got on that white horse myself. Now, no matter where I go or what I do, I know everything will be all right, because *I am* there.

What a relief!

> *Nothing can disturb the calm peace of my soul.*
>
> —J. KRISHNAMURTI

A Meaning and Purpose for Life

After losing the custody of my children and finding out I had cancer a second time, I had a choice to make: live or die. It was clear to me that to hold onto the pain of that loss would destroy my health and I would die. This I knew. So, once again, I made the choice to live. I made a choice to have faith in God that someday I would have an understanding and that everything would make sense to me. I determined that I would live each day grateful for the gift of life, having faith in God's divine plan and praying that the purpose of my life be revealed to me.

I remembered a scene from my life when I was unhappy within myself, when, surrounded by my children, I had watched the movie, *It's a Wonderful Life*, starring Jimmy Stewart. In the movie, which perhaps some of you have seen, Jimmy Stewart's character, facing financial disaster, contemplates suicide by jumping off a bridge, doubting the meaning of his life and muttering, "I wish I'd never been born." Clarence the angel is sent down from heaven to review his life from another perspective, showing him that his life did indeed have a meaning and a purpose. At the end of the movie Stewart's character realizes that love is the most important thing in life, that his life holds meaning and purpose, and that he is joyful just to be alive.

I remember seeing that movie and wishing inside myself that I knew for sure that my life had meaning and purpose.

Be careful what you wish for!

In my longing to find an inner answer, I found myself alone, facing the responsibility of my life. The responsibility for just my life! It was the first time that, instead of focusing on others, I was forced to focus on my own life for my own sake. It was only at this time, knowing that my life and health depended on it, that I allowed myself to take on the responsibility for my life. I made a conscious choice to have faith and live.

I began meditating every day, taking long walks and repeating affirmations aloud to myself, affirmations of health, faith and prosperity. As I walked, taking in the warm sunshine and the beauty of nature, I would say affirmations to discipline my mind and calm my emotions.

As I walked, chanting my affirmations, neighbors would nod and smile at me in passing. I let go of what others were thinking about me and focused my love, support and attention on myself. Gradually, my life changed. As I honored my feelings, disciplined my mind and placed healing affirmations of health and prosperity in my thoughts, my reality changed. I began to realize that my new state of mind was beginning to manifest in my outer world! My health improved, and my life began to change as I marshalled body, mind and spirit together for perfect health and inner harmony.

As time passed, my life changed totally. An amazing transformation had taken place—inside of me! That transformation manifested itself in miraculous ways each day, convincing me that my own inner being, my powerful mind and will were creating my life. I realized that my own thoughts, feelings and beliefs about myself were creating my destiny.

Deep inside, I reached a source of unconditional love, peace and joy that was totally untouched by the pain and tragedy of my life. This source was of total renewal and strength. I drank of the inner purity, beauty and peace of this heaven within. The joy and unconditional love was who I am! The authentic self! What joy and freedom I found in this realization.

My dear friends, I am talking to you of the human spirit. This spirit remains undaunted, ever joyful, loving and powerful within each one of us.

It was this spirit that made me choose life again and again, caused me to get up each time I fell with courage and faith, and caused me to rollerskate down the corridors of the hospital to my radiation treatments the first time I had cancer!

Find that spirit within yourself! Make a commitment right now to find out what it means to love yourself. To love yourself, you must first honor your feelings and, second, support what you feel. What does this mean? The next chapter explores what it means to find and honor your true feelings.

Affirmations:

- I love and accept myself exactly as I am, and I am taking care of me.

- I am healthy, strong and free of all illness.

- As I love and support myself, so does God and the Universe support me.

- Golden opportunities are everywhere for me.

- My courageous stand for health is calming my emotions and healing my body.

Exercise:

Practice sitting in front of a mirror. Look into your own eyes. What are you feeling? Are you critical of yourself? Angry? Guilty or fearful?

Say aloud: "I know you are feeling _____. I love you and I accept you just the way you are, and I am taking care of you."

Rest for a moment in that love. Feel the healing energy move through you. Make a choice to relax and be at peace.

3

*How Can I Have Feelings When I Don't Know
What It Is I'm Feeling? How Can I Have Feelings
When My Feelings Have Always Been Denied?*

—Song by JOHN LENNON

*Illness is dis-ease screaming through the body,
attempting to get the truth out, once and for all.*

—ANONYMOUS

The Voice of Illness

Without a doubt, most people I have met, whether seriously ill
or seemingly "healthy," are out of touch with their feelings. This
is an amazing reality. How can this be?

The simple truth of it is that as children we traded in our
honest feelings for the approval of the adults in our lives.
Because we were raised by adults who themselves had been
brought up in families that, as John Bradshaw would say, are
"shame-based," and incapable of the unconditional love we so
desperately need, we begin as little children (or in some cases
as infants) to feel unacceptable as we really are, and we start to
behave for the approval of the powerful adults who control our
lives. In doing this, in losing who by very nature we are, we
become very *angry*.

After losing our authentic selves, we then live in *fear*.

Guilt and *shame* lay deep beneath the surface.

We begin to emulate and incorporate the adults in our lives
and become controlling and critical, judgmental of ourselves
and others.

If so many of us are indeed blocked up, and I do mean blocked up, by these negative emotions, how can we feel any true emotions at all?

These repressed and denied negative feelings, having no release and remaining utterly suppressed, have got to lodge somewhere, and this is what I mean by blockages—these feelings then become blockages in our body that with time manifest as serious illness.

We can find out what we feel only by cultivating body awareness. That means, simply, that we must get in touch with the buried wisdom of the body. Only by ferreting out the negativity and releasing it can we find out what it is we truly feel.

All illness is a voice contacting you with a valuable message that you need to know about yourself. Find out what your body is telling you through what Bernie Siegel calls the "voice of illness."

Louise Hay, author of *You Can Heal Your Life*, has made a marvelous contribution in her catalog of the various illnesses and their emotional roots. I have found her discoveries in most cases to be true to the mark and a valuable guide to developing body awareness.

When we manifest the illness of cancer, our intellectual mind, the voice of what we "SHOULD DO," has become separate from our body, the voice of what we FEEL, what we want to do. In essence, what our body is saying to our mind is, "If you don't listen to me and honor what I feel, I'm going to divorce you."

A woman with breast cancer came to see me regarding an itchy, irritating rash that had spread over her body and persisted despite any ointment or medical treatment she applied. The woman tried everything, but still the painful rash persisted.

This woman was a well-known and highly-respected member of her community. She had received many awards honoring her achievements in society. I relaxed her and we began the inner journey of exploration. She took the feeling of the rash out of her body and sat it in the chair in front of her.

She was perplexed and then amazed to see a black, disgruntled image curled up on the chair. The face of the figure was hidden in shame and could not be seen. With gentleness and careful coaxing, we urged the figure in the chair to turn so that she could view the face. Tears poured from her eyes as she saw her own face as a child, miserable and filled with shame, her body curled up helplessly on the chair.

As we explored her childhood, it became clear that there was a small, frightened child within her, filled with shame and self-loathing. The woman's many worldly accomplishments had done little to fill the painful void within.

We worked together every day, reviewing childhood incidents, releasing guilt, shame and anger, and filling the child within with love and comfort. As we did so, the rash, so violent and persistent, began to fade and lessen.

This courageous woman began to realize that whenever painful feelings of anger or sadness surfaced, she would deny them and unconsciously rub the painful, itchy areas on her skin.

She realized that her body would no longer allow her to deny the hurt and pain of her life. Her many awards and honors meant little without her own feelings of self-esteem and self-worth. In the final analysis, it is how we feel about ourselves that is of value.

As Jesus said, "What shall it profit a man, if he shall gain the whole world, and lose his own soul."

As you take the time to look within and find out what it is you do feel, you can then honor your feelings and speak your truth in life. Speaking your truth takes courage and self-esteem. It takes a firm commitment of love to yourself that what you feel is valid and worthy. It takes stepping out of fear to speak and act in a manner that affirms confidence and integrity.

"The Confidence of Innocence" (*J. Krishnamurti*)

On my own path, I remember the intense fear I felt after being diagnosed with cancer. My reality was total panic and fear. In those days, I was afraid of people, afraid to pick up the phone to make a call.

In despair, I asked God to help me. I asked God to speak through me, act through me, and be present within me at all times. I began to ask for God's help in everything I said or did. In this manner, I began to feel the presence of God's help at every moment of my life. As time went on, I felt a sense of protection, safety and comfort that surpassed anything I had ever felt before. A confidence began to permeate my being, the confidence of innocence and trust, a true belief in myself.

After I founded Self-Healing, I was asked to introduce Bernie Siegel at a lecture he was presenting in Naples, Florida. The lecture was a sellout, with every seat taken, and the audience was an expectant sea of faces. All day long I had been wrestling with what I would say. For weeks, any attempt I would make to sit down and prepare a speech had been blocked from within. An inner command demanded that I go up unprepared and speak. My rational mind was sounding an all-out alarm, but a quiet source within me persisted and remained unmoved. My fear began to surface. What was wrong with me? How could I be so insane as to go before that large crowd of people unprepared? Yet, underneath it all, I felt a persistent calm.

Just before I was about to go on stage, I spoke with Bernie in the green room and voiced my fear. He smiled and said calmly, as if what I was doing made perfect sense, "Just let it go to God. You'll do fine." He told me of the first time he had ever just let go of his notes and spoke directly to the crowd; he described the freedom of the experience.

When I appeared on stage, I felt my knees knocking together as I looked out upon that sea of expectant faces. I let go of my ego and spoke with true feeling about my life, my work, and Bernie's influence on my life. I spoke with feeling from the heart. In spite of my fear, as I spoke my truth, I felt something within me "free up" and expound with confidence and joy. I did it! I was so proud of myself! Since then I have spoken many times and given workshops with larger and larger groups of people. Each new opportunity is a thrill and an adventure.

It takes risk and courage to break through fear. Once you do, the rewards are limitless.

Why should we live our lives boxed up in isolation within ourselves, without ever getting to truly know anybody, or allowing anyone to truly know who we are? Our whole lives can go by living in this insane, lonely manner.

In the first year of my practice, God felt I needed to realize this important lesson, so he sent me a young woman with advanced breast cancer who wanted my help to die. That was all she asked of me, just help to find inner peace so that she could die peacefully.

But I was new at my work and the name of my practice was Self-Healing, so I determined that I would help this beautiful woman find a reason to live. I did not realize at that time that death can also be a true healing.

I worked with this woman three hours a day, three times a week, and talked with her about every facet of herself and her life. I grew very close to her and loved her very much. It was very painful for me to see the loneliness of her life, her estrangement from her family, and her failing health. As time went on, she became frail and weak and could no longer come to my office, so I drove out to her home and sat with her as she lay in her bed, dying.

Still, I fought for her life. The very last words she spoke to me, with a smile and a sigh, were, "Oh, Angela, you're a pip!"

After her death, I attended a memorial held in her honor. There were hundreds of people present. The minister gave a speech about her life. As he was speaking, I thought, "Who is he speaking about?" This was surely not the woman I knew and loved. I looked around the church and had the awareness that of all the people there, I was the only one who really knew who she was.

This was a tremendous awareness for me. I learned two valuable lessons from my dear friend. First, to honor the needs and feelings of others. People know deep within themselves what they need to learn and how they feel. My dear friend's journey on earth was over. She had more valuable lessons to learn in other realms and needed to transcend this earthly plane. Second, I determined that I would honestly share my experiences and feelings with others so that I might get to know them, and I would open up and allow them to know me as well. Only in this manner can we live a full and joyful life.

Pretending to be perfect and above it all does not allow people to truly get to know you. It does not allow you to reach out for the support and love you need in order to be happy.

None of us are perfect, but real love means taking the risk to open up and be vulnerable. Love melts all the barriers that isolate us and separate us from one another. Allow love to fill you with the courage it takes to be fully alive. You are so worth it. This is the message of this story.

In our relationships with others, we must learn how to love and assert our intelligence, helping if necessary, and then to let that person go. This is honoring the paths of others and giving them a message of love that tells them you believe in them. Honor your own feelings, fill your own cup, and your love will overflow onto all those who cross your path. Each one of us is unique, and we are all at different stages of growth, development and awareness. It is my true belief that we are all in this "earth school" to learn what it means to love and know God. We are all connected at a deep level. Somewhere within ourselves, apart from our rational minds, is a source of being that *knows*.

Robert F. Gilley, a man with lymphoma, given by his doctors a two percent chance of survival, and who through visualization, meditation and inner work is now a healthy man, has said that cancer is "an obstruction of the soul's flow."

Dr. Carl Simonton states that in recent years doctors have discovered a nerve receptor on top of each white blood cell in the body. This means that the nervous system triggers the powerful immune system function of healing the body. Thus, if we are blanketed by negative emotions such as guilt, resentment or fear, this stress is going to impair the immune system from functioning properly. In this way, cancer cells have a chance to proliferate.

In getting in touch with our feeling selves, releasing negative emotions and finding the inner source of unconditional love and peace, we are sending a message of unconditional love to every cell of our body. We are giving our bodies and ourselves, as Dr. Bernie Siegel would say, "a *live* message."

We give the powerful immune system the opportunity it needs to flow through our bodies, healing us.

The Healing Power of Tears

Have you ever reflected upon the miracle of tears? In the amazing magnificence of our humanness, God has granted us the heavenly release of human feelings through the expression of tears. Have you ever tasted a tear? It is salty, coming from the ocean of feelings within. Tears are sacred reminders of our divinity. Without them, what would we do? We would become boarded up, rigid, unfeeling human beings.

Yet, how many of us allow the tears to freely flow—whether of sadness, suffering, ecstasy or joy? We cry when we are *moved* from within. Yet how many of us feel comfortable enough to let go when we feel tears spring to our eyes? In point of fact, many of us have learned numerous body tricks to prevent the release of tears. Biting our lips, stiffening up the jaw, we would do anything rather than risk the embarrassment of revealing ourselves as feeling human beings.

I was once this way. As a child, I made a decision never to allow anyone to see me cry. Of course, I was not aware that I had made this choice. It was just a natural result of being shamed as a child when I had cried.

While I lived up in the woods in Canada after manifesting the illness of cancer, I realized the *need to cry*. I hadn't cried in ages. One night the universe afforded me a magnificent opportunity when I turned on the television and there was a production of—*Madame Butterfly!* I let go and wept buckets! The refinement and honoring of sensitive human feelings in the opera made me aware of how barren and stoic my life had become. It was literally a joy to cry. I could actually feel my body heaving in relief and comfort.

Even after starting my work in Self-Healing, I felt uncomfortable witnessing my clients' release of sadness through tears. I would try immediately to comfort them to stop the release of pain. Then I realized what I was doing and took stock of myself. I had to **learn to honor another's pain. I had to learn to accept that the people I loved would sometimes feel uncomfortable or in pain. I had to let others be responsible for, and own, their pain.**

This was a tremendous healing for me, personally. Now I can hold another, while that person cries, in total love and acceptance, because I have learned to totally love and accept myself.

Now, in my workshops or lectures, when I observe people weeping, I feel good inside. I know that they are connecting with their feeling selves. I know that they are healing inside, healing the pain of their lives. I know that in this way they will heal and grow, as I have.

I have learned to honor the magical healing power of tears as a resource to be used for healing and inner peace. Tears now express to me all the gifts inherent in healing: humility, truth, love, peace, joy and the honoring of our feeling selves.

As our tears must be allowed to flow to express our humanness, so must our souls flow freely within to allow us to experience the wisdom, guidance and LIFE of our creative source. This "soul's flow" gives us *flexibility* and allows us to become *fluid* in the movements, feelings and actions that keep us on our true path in life.

Relax now, and do a meditation to go within yourself, within your body, and find out just what it is you are feeling.

Exercise: Meditation on Body Awareness

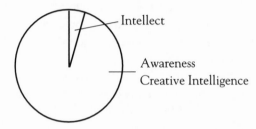

The intellect is only a very tiny part of who we are. This intellect, that was given to us by God as a "guardian," has turned into a guard that blocks us from experiencing our true selves.

Close your eyes and take a deep breath. . . . Let it out. . . . Feel your body relaxing. . . . Every breath you are taking is allowing you to feel more peaceful, more in touch with yourself, more relaxed. . . . There is nowhere you need to go right now, nothing you need to do. . . . The moment is now to focus on yourself, to go deeply within to a source of unconditional love and peace. . . . There is nothing to fear on this journey, nothing you need to do, just breath in a deep sense of peace and serenity as you relax your body. . . . Feel your mind slowing down as your body relaxes. . . . Visualize any thoughts you are having as messages written in the sand. . . . Now allow a deep inner source to wash away these messages in the sand as you slip deeply inside yourself, knowing there is nothing to fear, that you are completely safe. . . . You are going inside yourself to a source of love, peace and healing as your body relaxes.

Explore your body for any discomfort or pain. . . . If there is illness present, feel yourself going deeply within that part of your body, fearlessly exploring the feeling of discomfort, pain, or illness. . . . What does it feel like in this part of your body? . . . Describe the feeling. . . . Is there color present? . . . Allow yourself to visualize the color of this area of your body.

Now, *bring the feeling of that area of your body outside you, and sit it in a chair in front of you.* . . . What do you see? . . . Does this object have texture, color? . . . Ask the object to speak with you. . . . Tell it you are listening, receptive to its message. Ask it to give you a message you need to know about yourself or your life. . . . Converse with it, asking any questions and listening for the answers. . . .

Now, thank your body for its valuable message. . . . Now, look again within and visualize a scene from childhood. . . . See yourself as a small child. . . . What kind of look is on your face? Are you at peace? Angry? Lonely or sad? . . .

Talk to the little child and ask him or her what feelings are being experienced. Be willing to pay attention and listen. Say to this little child,

"I Love you, and I accept you exactly as you are, and I am taking care of you."

Now thank yourself for taking this time to go within yourself to find out what it is you are feeling. . . . Allow yourself to begin again to surface into consciousness. . . . When you are ready, open your eyes.

Explore now the information you received from going inside yourself. What is it you are feeling? Oftentimes it is the same familiar set of feelings you have been feeling since childhood, only now the scenes and players have changed.

Explore the information offered to you by your body. What is your body trying to tell you? Validate the information you are given and incorporate it into your day for inner peace and healing. Write it down; *believe it.*

Affirmations:

- I love and accept myself as I am.
- I accept all my feelings, even the negative ones.
- In this acceptance I pass through the negative into the positive.
- In this acceptance there is love.
- The love heals me and allows me to grow.
- I accept other people as they are with all their imperfections.
- I accept myself.
- In this acceptance my Iron Will of Ignorance relaxes, and I accept the Will of God.
- I emerge from this painful demanding ego into the light of God where there is humility, acceptance, love and peace.
- Acceptance is the key for me today.

4

Love knoweth no laws.

—John Lyly, *Euphues*

All, everything I understand,
I understand only because I love.

—Leo Tolstoy, *War and Peace*

Most people live lives of quiet desperation.

—H. D. Thoreau

The Priority to Love

A Love Story

What of this "obstruction of the soul's flow," as Robert Gilley called cancer? What does that mean?

I have found cancer to be a vehicle through which we can redirect our lives. Just as I needed to know that my life had a meaning and a purpose, many of us hold within us a cherished hope or dream that demands to be realized.

Cancer commands us to restructure our lives and review our priorities. It takes an act of will to initiate that first step toward change.

In my intimate work with my fellow human beings, the theme of love surfaces as a top priority. Let me illustrate to you what I mean.

I first met Ann when she attended my cancer support group with her husband and then later grew to know and love her in the few sessions we had together at my office where she confided to me the pain and sadness of her secret life.

Ann had a beautiful inner quality, one I can describe only as spiritual, and a faraway romantic look in her eyes. She possessed a depth of feeling and empathy that were rare gifts and a smile that glowed from deep within herself. Yet that smile was touched with a longing I could not understand or identify. So often, in the course of group interaction, her eyes would seek mine, searching, now I know, for the trust she needed to confide in me the innermost feelings of her heart and mind.

She sought and found in me the love and wisdom her gentle nature required and the unconditional love and acceptance that were necessary to her peace of mind. For you see, Ann had breast cancer. As her trust in our relationship developed, she gradually revealed the details of her life to me.

Many years before, when Ann was a young woman in her early twenties, she had fallen in love with a free-spirited young man, Philip, who released in her a depth of feeling that frightened and unsettled her. The pair were opposites; she came from a repressed background with a dominating mother, and he was a bit on the wild side, courageous and true to his feelings. Ann's mother disapproved of the relationship and exerted a powerful influence on Ann, who was already frightened of the out-of-control feelings Philip aroused in her.

Ann made a decision based on reason and ended the relationship. She married another suitor who represented comfort and security. Philip was heartbroken, but with a show of spirit and determination left the small town to find his path in the world. He became a successful man, married and divorced twice, but through the many years he never forgot about Ann. His love for her never diminished or faded; it seemed an unquenchable flame.

The passage of time did not alter Ann's feelings for Philip either. Though she raised children and performed the duties of wife and mother, deep inside her existed a secret longing for a life she could only dream of with a man she truly loved.

Over the years, they maintained contact with each other periodically through phone calls and at one point in a rendez-vous where they declared their feelings of deep love for one another. The passion was not physically consummated.

As Ann revealed her story to me, her eyes sparkled with life and happiness. Then she cried as if her heart would break with guilt and sadness.

All throughout the forty years of the relationship, she had never confided her secret to another living soul. The guilt and sadness of her life's decision finally manifested in the illness of cancer.

I helped Ann release her guilt and told her that love could never be a source of guilt but was always a gift from God. I encouraged her to let go to this love and see where it would lead her.

A week later she came to see me with a bouquet of beautiful gardenias. Gardenias were the favorite flower of my grand-mother, whom I dearly loved, and have a special significance for me.

Ann's face was glowing as her physical health was failing. I knew she had made a decision. She affirmed to me that this was so. She said that in letting go to the love she felt, she was experiencing a deep sense of inner peace and serenity. We further discussed the details of Ann's repressive childhood, the dominating influence of her mother, and her lack of confidence in making the crucial choices necessary to her own happiness and well being. In making this choice to love, Ann surrendered to her feelings and found inner peace. She said she could now leave this earth in her faith that love is eternal and that somehow her path would lead her home. She expressed faith that somehow she and Philip would find each other, perhaps in another realm, another time.

Shortly thereafter, Ann left Naples to return to her home in the North. I received this letter from her:

Dear Angela,

Before leaving for so many months away, I must express to you my gratitude for the beauty and joy and the realization of God's Love which you have helped manifest in my life!

When I look back on the spiritual encounters in my life, I realize that we are carefully led along the pathways of life—that there is a divine plan—and that the more we open ourselves to it, the more we are filled with His ever-flowing gifts of Light, Life and Love.

What a joy it is to know you and to learn from you! It also is so very evident that there is linkage—hindsight is great!

In the words of Thomas Merton, "The whole of life is in truth one continuous mystical experience because it has always been suffused with God's Love."

Angela, if anything should happen to me, if I should leave this earth—would you send a note to Philip—

Thank you, Angela, for assuring me that it is Good To Love.

Shalom and Love,

Ann

Thoreau said most people lead lives of "quiet desperation."

I have found the theme of repressed or lost love to be a recurring theme in cancer.

A few months later, I was notified of Ann's death. I wrote to Philip and shortly afterward received a call from him. He was a deeply sensitive and expressive man. He said that Ann's love for him had made him special, that he had always wanted to go forward in their relationship, but that Ann's background had made it impossible for her to have the confidence in herself she needed to fulfill her cherished dreams of life. He said that after she married he would have done nothing to hurt her or destroy her life; he only wanted the best for her. He asked me in what month she had died, saying he had felt her presence leave this earth at a certain time. It was the exact time she had died.

We concluded our conversation with the moving thought that he would find Ann in all the beauty of nature and life—the colors of the sunset, a raindrop on a green leaf. In all the awe, magic, pain and beauty of life, there he would find his "sweet-heart," in this feeling of love and beauty they would remain eternal, as one, forever—and nothing could ever destroy the strength and comfort of that love.

Before Ann's death, she confided that Philip had sent her a poem based on the feelings he had while gardening, when a small bird had perched beside him on a branch, cocking its head at him in a meaningful way. He had immediately felt the presence of Ann, and wrote these lines:

THE VISITOR

Did you travel far, wee thrush?
Yea, from the sea away—
From the pond, from the sand—
From the bayberry bush.
'Tis a place I know—

Oh, gentle bird, you wandered far indeed!
From tear to tear, scar to scar,
Heart to heart, breast to breast,
Need to need—

Tell me, brave wee friend,
What message does she send?
"From beginning to beginning—
From love to love—
From life to life—
There shall be no end."

Give her this then from me:
"From touch to touch—
Healing to healing—
From Time to Time—
Forever yours, forever mine.
Praise God!"

How does this story make you feel? Sad? Ridiculous? Do you want to take this book and throw it against the wall in moral outrage? Or does something within you resonate in empathy, compassion and truth?

What is going on inside you underneath what you have been taught or conditioned to believe? What are your real feelings about yourself and your life?

When you close the door of your room and are alone, without distractions of any kind, what do you think about? What are your priorities in life? What are you feeling?

Do you take the time or opportunity to go within yourself in privacy and silence and find out?

Our tremendous fear of life and love prevents us from leading a truly authentic life. The guilt and shame of childhood, when left unresolved and unhealed, prevents us from trusting enough in the flow of life in order to honor our innermost feelings and risk being who we are.

We allow the opinions and criticisms of others to become more crucial to our well-being than our very feelings about how our life is to be lived in the richest manner possible, according to our valued belief in ourselves.

In this superficial way, we lose our path in life and lose our authenticity. A whole life can be lost, lived unconsciously in hidden suffering, enslaved by the fear of what others might think should we step forward into reality, act on what we truly feel is valuable, and take charge of our lives.

As the husband of a woman with breast cancer wrote me after her death:

> As we shuffled towards the bathroom door she stopped and looked at me. "I now know why I have treated you so badly in the past few years. I resented you always being away." I felt as though I had been stuck by lightning. For nearly seventeen years of marriage and many months before we were married, I was away travelling. It was part of the deal. We entered into our marriage with this as a condition—a basic tenet. How could she resent this? If there was one thing that came from the therapy and

provided me with some serious, tangible insight it was this. Our relationship was not what either of us had hoped it would be in recent years, even before the breast cancer. Here it was—the answer. We both had been conditioned to accept our situation and not challenge it. Through your help she had unlocked a secret passage—a revelation. This one simple glimpse into our past had revealed a lot of answers to me. It continues to serve as a basis of understanding for me.

The first time I had cancer, I remember feeling that finding out what love was, was more important to me than bread or water. A song was popular at that time: "I Want to Know What Love Is." It became the theme song of my life.

Inside I was starving, trapped in a feelingless marriage, afraid to break away and risk the unknown. Guilt and fear were seemingly insurmountable. I was dying.

The realization of death propelled me into action to fight for my life. No longer could I deflect the crucial choices neces-sary not only to survive, but *to live*.

I broke free and took responsibility for my happiness. I was worth it! Since then, I have never looked back. No longer do I live "in quiet desperation" but in love, joy and freedom.

Please, do not let fear hold you back from finding out what it means to truly love. Start now to validate your feelings by writing them down. Take a look inside and get to know yourself. Only in this way can we truly understand and love anyone else.

You Are the Wizard

In the *Wizard of Oz*, the three heroes are subjected to all manner of trials and evil. They are on their way to visit the all-knowing wizard who will have the answers to help them.

When reaching Oz, they are devastated to see that the wizard is an illusion. In essence, all he can offer is to *believe in them and affirm them.* He helps them to realize that the answers have been within them all along.

Their heroic acts and the love between them on their path—a love tested by trial and commitment—have shown them who they are.

The lion has proven himself courageous; the tin man, pure- and noble-hearted; the scarecrow, a master strategist; and Dorothy—well, Dorothy had the power to go "home" all along. All she had to do was close her eyes.

This is really what I want to say to all of you.

Look in the mirror. *You are the wizard.* Close your eyes and go within to find your power. Then open yourself to life.

The yellow brick road has led us all home to ourselves. What joy!

The tears of all the broken-hearted children of this earth have caused the healers to return home.

Love will save us all. It will heal our wounded spirits, mend our broken hearts and set us free to experience our true divine birthright—joy, unconditional love, freedom and happiness.

Do not settle for less. Why live like a beggar when a kingdom of riches can be yours?

Do make love a priority. Everything else turns to dust.

Look up at the night sky. Let the stars become your dia- monds, the earth your mother and friend.

Turn off the television and spend time with each other. Slow down enough to care. Love each other before it is too late.

Cancer is a disease of the spirit. Only connection with the energy of love is a lasting cure.

You don't have to have a life-threatening illness to realize that love is the most powerful force in the universe. I have seen the power of love heal the mind, the body, the heart and the spirit.

It is time to Love. With love you have the power to heal your life. Love will set you free.

Exercise:

Reflect on the meaning of this story. It is a lesson in choice. How can we make the choices necessary to enrich our lives, choices made on our own behalf, if we lack the self-esteem?

Remember, it is by the power and nature of our choices that we create our lives.

5

Nothing can disturb the calm peace of my soul.

—J. KRISHNAMURTI

Love is letting go of fear.

—G. JAMPOLSKY

Fear is projection into the future.

—J. KRISHNAMURTI

Perfect love casts out fear.

—THE BIBLE

Courage is resistance to fear, mastery of fear—
not absence of fear.

—MARK TWAIN

There Is Nothing to Fear, *Including* Fear Itself

Converting Fear Into Power and Energy

Let's talk about fear, because fear is an actual energy that can be converted into a positive force for personal growth and health.

What are the causes of fear? **Fear is the mind's projection into the future.**

One of my great discoveries is the realization that in many cases, *yawning* is a manifestation of fear or resistance. Try to become *aware* the next time you find yourself yawning. What is it you are feeling? What has just been said? What feelings have you just experienced in your relationship to yourself or another? It is just amazing how many times you will find yourself *yawning* as fear or resistance arises within, with the resulting desire to descend into unconsciousness, or sleep.

A man I was working with on prosperity issues asked me a question. He noticed that while reciting the Lord's Prayer at church, at the mention of, "Give us this day our daily bread," he would yawn every time! He began to reflect upon this awareness.

In our work together, we uncovered deep-seated feelings of worthlessness in regard to money and financial prosperity. This man had developed a pattern in business of reaching a certain point of abundance and material wealth and then losing it all. He had repeated this pattern several times. The last experience had resulted in divorce from a woman he dearly loved. It was time to look within for healing.

As a child he had watched his mother be taken away by ambulance because of emotional problems. His father was distant and removed. His wealthy family's home was haunted by ghosts of loneliness and suffering without support or resolution. He felt abandoned and powerless.

At thirteen, he was sent away to boarding school. He felt enraged, panic-stricken, abandoned. There was nowhere to turn.

His bond with his mother was emotionally unfulfilling but sealed with financial relief when he needed it. Money became the emotional bond to his mother that fended off deep anxiety and an abyss within of unworthiness and shame.

Money was love to him. It was his only link of "nurturing" with an emotionally unavailable mother.

As he realized the truth of these traumatic feelings, he began to give love and support to his inner child. He realized the need to be responsible for himself, emotionally and financially. The unhealthy bondage between his needy child self and his mother was healed through the understanding, love and support of his adult realizations.

As the guilt and shame of childhood was discovered, understood and released, he began to be aware of the resistance within himself to receive and succeed. As the inner child received love and support, my client was able to recognize the painful guilt and fear that sabotaged his success in life. In this way he grew empowered through awareness to change the destructive habits that were holding him back in life. He was able to own his right to prosperity and abundance and to change his life.

As I have mentioned to you, when I first had cancer, I had the awesome realization that fear was my master in every area of my life. This was a tremendous feeling of total powerlessness. I knew I had to take charge of my fear because it was destroying my life. But how to do that?

I began to ask God to enter my life at every moment. As I would pick up the phone to make a call, fear would fill my throat and block me. When I answered the door to greet another human being, or had a creative thought or vision, fear would come in and block me from going forward. Fear was my master. Sound familiar?

I began to ask God for help in every way: God, speak through me; God, act through me. I would then let go and trust to the help of God. I didn't know it then, but I was indeed letting go to God in every sense of the word; however, I didn't think of it that way. *It was the only thing that worked.* I asked God for help every moment of the day. I realized that my pride and guilt had prevented me from reaching out for the help and guidance I so desperately needed. I further realized that if we want help with something, we need to ask! This is a necessary part of a successful life. In this manner, we are exercising faith, trust, confidence and humility. God answers all prayers, sometimes not in the form we visualize, but an answer always comes; it is up to us to identify that answer, interpret it and receive it.

After working through fear in this manner every day in every way, I eventually reached a point were I viewed life through different eyes.

One night, I was driving through Naples. The stars in the sky seemed so precious and near; all the streetlights seemed beautiful. The world felt like a friendly, inviting place—the world was my oyster!

I was filled with wonder and joy as I realized that my perception of the world had greatly changed! No longer was I a powerless, cowered individual—I felt strong and capable, optimistic and adventurous. I had mastered my fear! What an exquisite feeling!

I would love to share with you a few methods I devised along the way that have helped me, so that you too can release your fear and become empowered. You can do it! I know you can. I have such faith in you, you who have the spirit, wisdom and fortitude to believe in yourself! The two exercises at the end of this chapter will help you.

As you choose each moment to think thoughts of love and trust, identifying your fears and converting them into positive affirmations, you are sending missiles of light and energy into the Universe. You are creating your world! Your boundless energy need no longer be wasted in negative thoughts; now you can *create* with that energy. Your creative force is your life force. It is sacred. Allow it to flow within you, guiding and transforming your life. Once you conquer fear, you move upward in life to a higher order of living and being. Go with the divine flow and open to receive the wonderful life that is yours to enjoy if you believe it, open to it, and allow it. The power lies within YOU.

If indeed we must live on this planet where predatory behavior is so much a part of Nature, doesn't it make sense to live your life in power and strength? The hero can laugh in the face of adversity. He can laugh because he is powered by a faith and belief in himself that is never daunted, a hope that burns eternally to know what miracle lies just ahead at the next turn of the road. A hero never gives up hope! Never! She makes the choice to laugh because it is a choice of empowerment, an affirmation of faith in herself and God and Life itself. God, the Universe and Life itself raise up the hero, giving him or her support in the most miraculous and unforeseen ways imaginable. I know this is so. I live it!

Exercise:

Part 1. Identifying Your Fears

First close your eyes and relax. Go within yourself. Feel the fear. Look at your fear. Visualize it as a gaily-colored butterfly floating within yourself. This butterfly of fear has favorite places where it loves to rest. Visualize these places as flowers rooted within yourself. These flowers have names on them. You can see these names. Identify your fears. Open your eyes, take a pencil and write them down on a piece of paper. You may want to use different colors of ink in writing down your fears and affirmations.

Chances are, your list of fears will look something like this:

- Fear of not having enough money
- Fear of losing your health
- Fear of death
- Fear of life
- Fear of failure
- Fear of losing someone we love
- Fear of not being good enough
- Fear of not being perfect
- Fear of change
- Fear of something bad happening, the other shoe dropping
- Fear of expressing feelings
- Fear of communicating honestly
- Fear of life on earth!

The list is endless. Why should we go on living in this manner, when we can make a choice right now, at every moment, to choose love instead of fear?

Part 2. Transforming Your Fears into Energy

Now, through the power of choice, we are going to turn these fears into Positive Affirmations of Faith. You have the power to do this because *you are in charge!*

Allow me to show you how to do it. Take each fear listed above and change it into an affirmation.

- God is the source of my supply. I open myself to the prosperity and abundance of the Universe, knowing I am worthy and deserve the best.

- My body is healthy, strong and free of all illness. As joy and hope flow through my being, I give my body a message of love, peace and vibrant well-being.

- God's Love is flowing through me, filling each cell of my body with energy and life. I am fully alive with health, love and joy.

- I open myself to the source of unconditional love and peace that exists within myself. There is nothing to fear. I am safe.

- I love and accept myself exactly as I am, and I am taking care of me. I enjoy my relationships in trust and love, fully alive within the moment. God protects and guides me and all those I love.

- I am good enough. I relax in the love and acceptance of myself. I rejoice in my humanness.

- As I love and support myself, so does God and the Universe support me.

- I give up my resistance to change. As the seasons change in beauty, grace and dignity, so do I move forward effortlessly into the flow of life, knowing I am on my way to my highest good.

❧ The light of my inner journey is transforming my perception of life. I handle all experiences with trust, ease and intelligence. All experiences teach me how to empower myself in life and go forward through the doors God opens for me to my higher good.

❧ My feelings are my only reality. I am free to express myself and find out who I am.

❧ There is nothing to fear in speaking my truth with care and confidence. In this manner, I express my self-esteem and love in all my relationships. I do not deny the negative feelings, and I see them as pathways to health and inner peace. As I release the negative, I make room for joy love, peace and healing.

Now look at your two lists. They represent two states of mind. There are only two states of mind: Doubt and Fear, or Love and Trust. Take your pick! The choice is entirely up to you, because *you are in charge*.

> **Things do not have to make sense rationally
> in order to work out in divine right order and
> to be the right direction for you.**

Heeding the Inner Voice

I wrote this passage seven years ago entitled: "Who or What am I Following?"

About ten years ago, I was lying on my bed, deep into the high drama of my life, when I heard, as clearly and succinctly as one can hear anything, a voice calling, "Help!"

The voice, shocking in its clarity, intensity and sincerity, indeed, shocking in its absolute reality, sounded like the voice of a very shy person, either drowning or smothering, who, unaccustomed to shouting or similar displays, had plucked up her last mouthful of air and choked out a final heartrending plea.

Or, more finely drawn, the voice was that of a person dreaming a dreadful dream and, frozen to the spot, cannot scream and finally does. A voice ripped from the depths of my being.

"Help," cried the voice from the depths. And then again, "Help!"

I heard that voice and have been following it ever since.

Before that time I had been following someone else's voice. That hadn't worked out very well, but that voice had been a lot louder than my own, and had just about silenced mine. Consequently, the garbled, tormented, but clear as a bell voice, honed to a fine point, the message echoing alarmingly throughout my consciousness.

I have never forgotten that moment.

You might call it a spiritual awakening, for since that time, I have tried to still the babblings and flutterings of everyday existence, and find time enough to listen to myself.

If I have a problem to solve, I take the time to lie back, close my eyes, and get in touch with the source of energy that is I. Simple faith is what it is. As I pray to God to give me strength and guidance, I once again traverse the path back to where I live. The simple, tender child that knows her own likes and dislikes, her own desires and beliefs, and the answer to all the problems of my life. The sweet source of I, that once held out her arms to me, pleading with me to save myself.

I realize now this faith of mine gives every day a sense of sparkle and zest. I never know what surprise is in store for me; or just when all seems lost, what hero will step in to save the day.

Should a day evolve that stifles the child within me, then all life smacks of meaninglessness, and my arms and legs motor along without the spirited driver to guide their way.

So it comes down to a choice I make every day. I am a believer. What, you ask me, am I following? I answer truthfully: I follow humbly the child within; with the help of God I am following myself.

Take a risk. Open yourself to change. Make that leap of faith. Ever since I turned my life around with the help of God, I have been making choices based on deep feeling and intuition. I weigh these choices with the valid information given to me by my rational thought processes. Sometimes, in making tough decisions, I have gone against the cautions of my rational thought and made powerful choices from the heart. These choices have never failed me and have transformed my life at crucial points in directions I could never have carefully thought out, foreseen or imagined. I see, upon careful reflection, that these choices are made with the help of my Inner Voice.

Only through meditation, relaxation, and inner work can we keep in touch with that gentle yet all-commanding inner voice that keeps us on our path in life. This Inner Voice is an unrelenting, persistent feeling about what we Must Do, and often is in conflict with our rational mind, which is always telling us what we Should Do.

Get in touch with your Inner Voice and believe in it, and it will never steer you wrong.

For most of my life, I ignored this inner commander and listened to the advice and judgment of others, whose ways were violent and cruel. My inner voice was so gentle that I interpreted it as being weak. Now I know that tension and violence are weaknesses. Gentleness, love, kindness and understanding take tremendous strength and an Unbending Will for the Good. This Unbending Will for the Good is nothing less than the Divine Will within each one of us. This Divine Will is totally different from what I call the Iron Will of Ignorance, which rules so many of us.

Have you ever met anyone, or noticed in yourself, an unbudging, unyielding will that, when exercised, seems to result only in misery, suffering and destruction? Most of us cling to this Iron Will of Ignorance as though our lives depended on it. As a result, our lives lack intimacy, warmth, love, kindness and truly benevolent feeling. In clinging to this unbending, unchanging

Will, we must have our way at all costs. So often we have pyrrhic victories, leaving ourselves and those we love shattered and destroyed, and our life in ruins around us.

Why live this way? It doesn't make any sense! Arouse and awaken within yourself your Divine Will for the Good. This Will is un-bending for the Good and its action results in harmony and inner peace. In making crucial choices, pray to God for help and guidance. Let go of your Iron Will of Ignorance and pray instead, "Thy Will Be Done." "Thy Will Be Done." You will find within yourself an amazing resistance to this surrender! Flow through the fear and resistance and get in touch with the Divine Will within. Watch your health and life transform toward the higher and better.

After I had been in practice about a year, I was deeply troubled by the negative circumstances of my second marriage. My partner was in denial of his alcoholism. My feelings were being denied and ignored. I was up against the Iron Will of Ignorance right within my own life and marriage! As much as I tried to smooth things over and work them out, my life became a battleground of chaotic behavior and financial disasters. I now know this life of turmoil is part of the disease of alcoholism. My feelings of gratitude toward my second husband fast dissolved in the stubborn will for chaos and ignorance that had become my life with this person. I prayed and prayed to God for help and guidance in the situation.

One night, drained and weary, I returned home. As I drove up the driveway, I was praying to God for help. I had no money at all, none! For about six months I had been trying to follow the guidelines of Mother Theresa and run Self-Healing on a donations only basis. I had not received a single donation!

My husband's finances were a total disaster. His brother and sister-in-law were visiting with us and he had promised there would be no drinking. Without any money, how could I extricate myself from this unhappy marriage and go forth in life? The problems seemed insurmountable.

I prayed to God for help, my head resting on the steering wheel of my car. All at once I heard a voice say to me, "Look at the birds of the air, they neither toil nor do they spin, yet your heavenly Father takes care of them. How much more so, you?" Not being well versed in the Bible, I was astounded by the clarity and profundity of these words.

When I walked into the house, the empty beer cans testified that all promises had been broken and life was going on as usual in accordance to the Iron Will of Ignorance!

I made the decision that night to leave my marriage and acted on it. My sister-in-law supported me in that decision. As she was leaving, knowing I had no money, not one dime, she handed me fifty dollars and said, "This is just the start of all good things for you. God has a special plan for you, and you're going to get through this and have a wonderful life." To this day, I thank her for those beautiful words of support.

In the coming weeks, I took stock of my fears and began doing affirmations for financial prosperity. When worry set in, I would get up from my chair, leave the house, and take a walk in nature, saying my affirmations over and over again. There was no room for doubt or fear in the midst of all these positive affirmations. I was fighting for survival.

I began to charge for my services at Self-Healing. I realized that I had deep feelings of worthlessness in regard to financial prosperity and many negative beliefs concerning money. I released these beliefs and gave myself love, encouragement and support.

In only a few weeks time, I was working at full capacity. The phone was alive with prospective clients and new opportunities. I had released a major block within myself, taken a major risk, and moved forward one hundred percent into the flow of my life.

This very difficult decision proved to me once again beyond a doubt the amazing power within ourselves to direct and empower our destinies. Such decisions are never easy and are always made on the basis of an inner moral struggle. In freeing myself from a destructive relationship and affirming my right to have love, joy and prosperity in my life, the Universe had come forward in all its power and glory to assist me on my path.

This was nothing less than a miracle for me and affirmed to me that As I Love and Support Myself, So Does God and the Universe Support Me.

Have the courage to investigate this mysterious puzzle that is life on this earth and go forward, out of fear and into a new life, a new way.

Once, long ago, when I was living in the woods up in Canada, I walked down the dirt path to the flowing brook outside my door with a bucket in my hand. Having no electricity or plumbing, I was filling this bucket with water to bring back to the cabin for drinking and washing purposes. As I watched the beautiful pure waters cascading down the waterfall in the brook, I was struck by an awareness: "My life won't always be this way." I felt the comfort of this awareness. As I filled my bucket with fresh water, I noticed within the clinging green moss of the rock, little creatures holding fast to the surface of the rock, under the force of the cascading water, clinging on for dear life! As I peered closely, I noticed that every now and then, one of the creatures would "let go" and fall freely, swept away by the current of the water. I had an awareness: these creatures are just like us, human beings clinging fiercely with all our might to withstand the flow of life and maintain our ingrained, un-changing ways! And all we have to do is let go—and live!

Letting go of fear means letting go to love and joy and empowerment in your life. It is only your life we are talking about! Let go of fear and flow into the joy and wonderment that is yours to experience. You are worth it!

Exercise: Free Fall

Be aware of your breathing. I have found that many people have formed a habit of very shallow breathing. In becoming fearful individuals, we close ourselves off from inhaling the world around us. Oxygen kills cancer cells! Release all fear and partake deeply of the sacred breath of life!

I would like to share an experience with you at this point, a creative imagery that helps facilitate the process of letting go of the Iron Will of Ignorance. It is called Free Fall, and it is nothing more than a beautiful visualization that helps you to "Let Go" to the Divine Will.

The Journey
Feel your body relaxing. . . . Feel your mind beginning to slow down. . . . Every breath you take brings you deeper inside yourself, to a source of unconditional love and peace. . . . Every breath you take makes you feel more relaxed . . . more at peace within yourself. . . . It feels so wonderful just to lay back and to relax.

As you relax, visualize your thoughts as a flock of gentle lambs, and you are standing among the lambs with a magic wand. . . . In your hands this magic wand has the power to cause each of the little lambs to lay down to rest in the green pasture. You walk among the lambs touching each lamb in turn with your magic wand. . . . Each lamb gazes up at you with gentle, soulful eyes and then lays down to rest in the green pasture. One by one you subdue the beautiful little lambs with your magic wand until you alone are standing in command. . . . You alone are in charge and all the little lambs are at rest at your feet in the green pasture. Your mind is completely at peace. . . . In this feeling of peace there is freedom. Allow yourself to experience a sense of inner peace and freedom as your body deeply relaxes. . . .

Visualize within your heart a beautiful inner flame. . . . Your heart is made out of a hard, red wax. . . . As you breathe, your breath fans this inner flame of unconditional love and passion for life. . . . You can feel your heart softening as this beautiful flame grows brighter and brighter. . . . Your heart softens as this beautiful feeling of warmth and heat and energy melts your

52 • THE HEROIC PATH

heart, and you can feel your heart opening, and all the unconditional love and peace pouring forth from your heart and
flowing into all of your internal organs, giving you a message of
unconditional love and peace. . . . And this unconditional love
and peace is *who you are*. . . . You feel the warmth of this
beautiful radiation of love flowing through your inner self and
warming any frozen spaces within yourself. . . . You feel these
feelings coming alive again as the love for yourself warms your
being and melts all of your fears and reserves. . . . You feel this
warmth and energy warming you as you deeply, deeply relax. . . .
As you relax you feel this beautiful unconditional love. . . . You
feel it as a beautiful white light and within this beautiful white
light of joy and peace is your authentic self. . . . This white light
is *who you are*. . . . Relax into the experience of being who you
are. This white light of unconditional love and peace, joy and
acceptance is untouched by any of the pain of your life. . . . You
relax into this beautiful feeling of unconditional love and peace.
Relax into being who you are. . . .

Pause

Now, relaxing further, visualize within yourself the rushing
waters of a beautiful waterfall in a tropical paradise. . . . This
waterfall is tumbling down upon the beautiful cliffs within
yourself. . . . You see the green of the vegetation, the lush
ferns. . . . You visualize the waterfall as a beautiful, emerald
green. . . . You find yourself longing to climb to the top of this
beautiful, cascading waterfall. . . . You feel the rich earth beneath your feet as you climb to the very top and take in the
beautiful magic of this paradise and its lush green vegetation. . . .
You feel inner peace and serenity. . . . As the birds wheel in the
sky overhead, you feel yourself letting go and falling—falling—
falling in freedom. As you let yourself go, you visualize the cool,
green pool beneath you. . . . You free fall into an acceptance of
who you are. . . . Just as you near the bottom of the waterfall,
you feel a tropical breeze lift you up in the air. It lifts you higher

and higher; you feel the support of the universe and the support of God in this lush tropical breeze. . . . It lifts you higher and higher to the outer reaches of the universe. . . .

Pause

From this place, you look down at yourself, at your life on earth, and you feel your life from a new perspective. . . . Feel the serenity and the detachment of this point of view. . . . Feel how much freedom it allows you. As you do, feel yourself beginning to merge into a beautiful totality of being and to experience the wholeness and wonder of being who you are. . . . You experience a harmony of your body, mind and heart. Your body, mind and spirit are in perfect wholeness and order for healing and health. . . . Allow yourself to rest in the love of the experience of being who you are. . . . Feel yourself touching base within yourself, with your feeling self. . . . Feel the freedom of this experience. . . . Now bless yourself for taking this time for you. . . .

Pause

Allow yourself again, to begin to surface back into consciousness. . . . Know that you are honored, that you are worthy, and that you are loved. . . . When you feel comfortable and ready, open your eyes.

Relaxing the mind with tender, loving imagery allows us to touch base with our feeling self. The inner flame of unconditional love warms the heart, and opens us to receive gifts of grace and healing. As we let go of fear and free fall into acceptance, trust and love, we experience the divine support of God and are released into the flow of life in safety, protection and joy.

6

The past is the present, isn't it? It's the future too.

—Eugene O'Neill, *Long Day's Journey into Night*

That which is essential in life is invisible.

—Antoine d'Exupery, *The Little Prince*

The river laughed. Yes, that was how it was.
Everything that was not suffered to the end
and finally concluded, recurred and the same
sorrows were undergone.

—H. Hesse, *Siddhartha*

Only through awareness can we awaken from this
dream of sorrow and loneliness and find the
recognition and inner peace we so need and deserve.

—A. Trafford

The Invisible Child

As pointed out by John Bradshaw in his book, *Healing the Shame that Binds You,* and by so many other eminent contributors in this field, there is a little child within each one of us that is injured and in need of love and healing.

Within myself and in the course of my work, I made an amazing discovery. My inner child, and the inner child of so many of the people I have worked with, is not only injured, but also invisible. This little child longs to be recognized. The persistent theme of the Invisible Child's life is one of **disappointment**. Disappointment, when you decipher it, means to be *dis-appointed,* or thwarted, frustrated, dismissed and unrecognized. Has disappointment been a constant thread in your life and relationships? Then you are most likely harboring within yourself a lost, invisible child in need of rescue, love, comfort, attention, and recognition.

Within the past year of my work, while writing my autobiography, a startling memory surfaced into consciousness:

My friend Carol Ann and I are standing outside my house. Our heads are together, composing a letter to my mother and father. Inside, my parents are entertaining company. We write the letter:

"Dear Mr. and Mrs. Passidomo, we are sorry to inform you that your daughter Angela has cancer. There is nothing more we can do."

Sincerely,
Dr. Shomberg.

I quietly enter the house and place the letter on the kitchen table. Then I lie down on the living room floor, pretending that I am dead. My parents find the note and then enter the living room. They pretend not to notice me. I lie there a long while before finally bursting into tears of frustration and sadness.

My parents are surprised by my outburst. With all the duties and responsibilities of raising six children, they have no idea of the struggle for recognition within the heart of their middle child.

What has cancer to do with childhood? Supported by the findings of Dr. Carl Simonton, Dr. Bernie Siegel and so many others, my work and life have shown me many common denominators in the childhood of those manifesting the illness of cancer. They include:

• a sense of betrayal of trust in relationships at an early age
• the need to be perfect

- a persistent feeling of not being "good enough"
- a heavy burden of emotional and practical responsibility at an early age
- overwhelming feeling of responsibility and caretaking in childhood
- an inability to live life authentically with a healthy sense of self
- behavior for the approval of others
- inner feelings of suppressed resentment
- unhealthy guilt

The combination of many of these early life experiences leads to an unhealthy concept of self and an inability to unconditionally love oneself or others.

I have found, as well, an inner feeling of being victimized and a tendency toward martyr-type behavior with the expectation of love and eternal devotion as rewards. When the martyr-type behavior goes unrewarded and unrecognized, we then feel the familiar feelings of childhood surfacing: *guilt, disappointment, deep hurt and resentment.*

The truth of it is this: as children we experience a certain set of feelings. Even if these feelings are miserable, they become familiar to us. We then recreate these feelings all our lives in the destructive patterns we form and in the relationships we seek and nurture.

How then can we be released from this cycle of pain and sadness?

A woman came to me with breast cancer metastasized to the bones. She was seriously ill and could barely walk through the door of my office. Her doctor had told her, "You know what you have and you're going to die from it."

She came to my cancer support group and then began working with me a few times a week on a private basis. She was a Christian Scientist and her religious beliefs prohibited her from visualizing the cancer as an illness. We got around this by recognizing the fact that cancer cells exist in the body, so we guided her visualization toward eliminating the cancer cells.

Through relaxation and meditation techniques, we probed deeply into the subconscious mind. She communicated with her body, asking for valuable information through the "voice of illness." The first word her illness spoke to her was, "Ouch!"

As this woman changed her negative beliefs about herself, improved her relationships through expressing feelings and forgiveness, and focused valuable attention and love on herself, her health began to improve.

However, whenever it came time to get in touch with her inner child, she would show signs of resistance and distaste and was unable to visualize herself as a child. Her feelings toward her child-self were filled with shame and criticism. When it came time in our session to relax and connect with her inner child, she would scrunch up her nose and shift around on the couch in full-blown resistance.

With tenderness and love we sought communication with her inner child, but the child remained invisible.

Her health steadily improved as her resistance lessened, and one day, two years into the work, we connected with the voice of her inner child. The first thing the invisible child said was, "Ouch!"—then, "You found me!"

The connection between the voice of illness and the painful voice of the invisible child was undeniable. We began to work on releasing the childhood pain, hopelessness, guilt and anger, and on giving the child unconditional love and support.

Her courageous inner work reaped her the emotional rewards of unconditional love and inner peace, plus the miracle of healing. She is now well.

Such is the tremendous power of love in healing, and the importance of healing negative childhood beliefs about ourselves so that we may go forward in health in our lives.

A few years ago I was giving a speech from a church pulpit about a workshop I was preparing to do on "Finding the Authentic Self."

As I finished my speech and stepped down from the lectern, I was able to see a large crowd gathering at the back of the church where reservations were being taken for my workshop. As I walked to the back to speak with the throng of interested people a nagging doubt entered my mind. How was I going to have the endurance to handle such large groups of people? How would I have the courage and fortitude to go forward in confidence on the greater level being offered to me?

As these doubts were surfacing and I was engaged in conversation with a group of lively adults, I began to notice a small child at the edge of the group who was beckoning me to speak with him. So bright and full of life was he, it was hard to ignore him as he stood at my elbow and motioned to me that he had a secret to tell me.

I excused myself from the group and bent down so that he could whisper in my ear. "I liked what you said up there and I wanted to tell you something." He came closer and stared solemnly into my eyes. "I have a secret to tell you. I have INCREDIBLE STRENGTH. INCREDIBLE!"

He took my hand and brought me out the door of the church to the back, where he demonstrated his ability to crack in half a heavy piece of a dead, fallen tree. He then flexed his muscles in accomplishment.

I looked at this eight-year-old child in amazement. I thanked him and told him how special he was and how much he had helped me.

"I know." He smiled and skipped away into the milieu of church-goers.

I re-entered the church feeling humble and replenished. God had sent me an immediate answer in the form of this amazing little child. The message was clear: all the faith, energy, trust and strength I needed to go forward would be found within myself, in my powerful inner child.

How does a person come to have an invisible child? There are many causes:

- Shame
- The glaring spotlight of criticism
- A sense of powerlessness in dealing with overwhelming life situations.
- Painful humiliation
- Sexual abuse
- A sense of being controlled by powerful adults
- Feelings of worthlessness and inadequacy
- Emotional abuse
- Physical abuse

All these events and more can cause us as children to want to shrink into nothingness inside ourselves. Feelings of failure and lack of self-esteem can cause us as adults to withdraw into drugs or alcohol, or take the opposite extreme and become uncontrollable workaholics at the mercy of relentless Inner Drivers that prevent us from enjoying our lives.

Many years ago, when I lived in my log cabin in the woods, every Friday was bread baking day. I was proud of always having fresh home-baked bread available in my home instead of the store-bought variety. So every Friday morning I would wake up, my heart already pounding with dread, and prepare the yeast for softening in the bread bowl. I would get the fire going in the wood stove so the oven would be nice and hot. After a moment's hesitation, I would say to myself that three loaves of bread was not enough; while I was at it, I ought to double the recipe, then I would have enough to freeze. I would then increase the amount of yeast and transfer it to my largest bread bowl. Upon reflection, my mind would insist that I include some raisin bread, cinnamon rolls, some homemade donuts, and perhaps a recipe of Italian bread. Then I would double the recipe for the Italian bread! And look, I might as well use up those bananas and make some banana bread! This is a true story!

At the end of the day, my kitchen and dining room would literally be covered with dozens of loaves of bread, rolls and donuts, while I would be doubled up on the living room couch with a blazing headache, my neck and shoulders in knots of pain. I would drive myself all day long in this out-of-control, insane manner, without a moment of relief. I was my own worst enemy! After a period of time, I began to dread Fridays. When Friday morning dawned, my body was already tied up in knots before I could get up out of bed!

Like so many of us, I was at the mercy of myself. I did not know what it meant to be a balanced, healthy individual. I drove my body beyond its limits without giving it the care and attention I needed and deserved. I was invisible and unrecognized; I knew only how to serve and care for others, and I was deeply resentful and despondent.

Cancer showed me that I was going to die without ever having really lived.

Because of my unresolved childhood guilt and shame, I didn't have the slightest inkling of what it meant to love myself. I had to learn. It was hard cracking through those destructive old ways and changing, but I knew I had to do it, not just to survive, but to live.

Does this story ring a bell to you? Do you need to learn how to stop being your worst enemy and become your best friend? In getting to know yourself, you can find out where your destructive patterns originated and then release them, making room for healthy change.

When I realized that my inner child felt invisible, I made a list of the things I would do for a child I dearly loved and cherished. I realized I would dress this child in lovely clothes, style her hair and give her the love and attention she was dying for! It was painful to realize that I had never felt worthy enough to do these wonderful things for me! I began to take stock of myself—all my clothes were bargains; so few pieces were really me. I made a vow to dress myself and take care of myself in a manner that reflected caring and self-esteem. And you know what? I did it and continue to do so today, and I feel good about myself.

A few weeks ago, I was with my children at the local mall, when an unusual incident occurred. A little girl, catching my eye, left her mother's side and walked directly and purposely up to me, the tips of her shoes connecting with mine. I had to laugh. She was just so spontaneous and courageous and delightful. Her hair was done up in curls with pretty bows and fancy barrettes; her outfit was stylish and crisp; her little shoes and lacy socks a testament to attention and care. She gazed up at me without a glimmer of fear or hesitation and held up her arms to me, urging me to pick her up. This little girl was so obviously loved and cared for that I could not help but exclaim, "You are beautiful! Yes, you are!" She responded with delight, reaching up to me in that way children have when they want you to pick them up. Her eyes were bright with the courage of innocence.

I smiled at her mother and grandmother who were watching in amazement, trying to guide her away and saying, "She *never* does this, *never!*"

I picked the child up in my arms with permission from the mother, who was caught up in the excitement of the moment and nearly fainted when the little girl threw her arms around my neck and wouldn't let go! "I love you!" she laughed, embracing me, "I love you."

My children watched the scene, smiling. It was just another day at the mall with their mother.

At the time of this marvelous experience, I knew exactly what the Universe was conveying to me through the expression of this child.

Somehow this spontaneous, healthy, cared-for little girl represented my own loved and nurtured little child.

The little girl at the mall picked up on the energy of love within me and naturally responded. This is the way it works.

A man came to my support group with a question to ask me. He was suffering from rectal cancer; he had been in recovery from alcoholism for seventeen years. He said, "Why do I have the feeling wherever I go that people are lying to me? No matter where I go or what I do, I feel like saying, stop lying to me!"

I said, "You're right! People are lying to you! If you can find the truth within yourself and learn to express it, your world will change."

He began sessions with me on a private basis and drew me a picture of his inner child. He showed me the picture, an enraged, demonic child, that he nicknamed "Chuckie," after the diabolical doll in the horror movie.

I helped him release the anger and pain of Chuckie and get in touch with his needs. Chuckie had been invisible for a long time and was very angry. My client made a list of the things he needed to do to make his child visible. He began to be selective in his wardrobe and take care of his physical and emotional needs. He discovered in himself a wonderful sense of humor as well.

One evening, his wife took me aside after our group meeting and said, "He's gone too far with this Chuckie thing, way too far. Yesterday I opened the front door to get into the car and there was a child's car seat in the front seat. He told me I'd have to sit in the back; Chuckie was riding up front with him!"

Isn't that wild? The creative force that flows through us does indeed have a sense of humor. As this man healed, the picture of Chuckie changed into a heroic figure reflecting strength and inner peace, walking his path in life.

It is never too late to have a happy childhood! In the words of the Little Prince, "That which is essential in life is invisible to the eye."

Unconditional love of the child within is essential to healing our lives.

When you want to get in touch with your feelings, simply close your eyes and visualize your inner child. See the look on the little child's face. What is this child feeling? What does the child need? If you can take the time to relax and connect in this manner, you can find out what you are feeling at any given moment of time. That little child is **you**. Take the time now to give yourself the love and support so necessary for inner peace and happiness. You deserve it!

A woman with breast cancer metastasized to the liver began work with me on a private basis. She was filled with a deep sense of hopelessness about her life and many negative beliefs that blocked her self-esteem. She asked me, "What does it mean to love yourself?"

As we probed into her past, we discovered that as a child her father had identified her with his mother, who had died of cancer. Without realizing it, she had incorporated a fear of cancer, which had been whispered to her by her mother in hushed tones whenever the word was mentioned in the home. In addition, this woman told me initially that she had no real talents or abilities, that she was essentially very "mediocre." She was unaware that this was a conception she had formed of herself from receiving negative messages and criticism as a child. She felt unloved and unrecognized. As we probed further into the "voice of illness," we discovered that cancer was the only recognition this woman had ever known. Through cancer she had received some of the attention she had been needing since childhood. For this reason, she was amazed to find within herself an unwillingness to release the illness. She had to learn how to express her feelings in her relationships and develop a sense of self-esteem before she could "let go" of her illness. Cancer had made this woman visible.

This very wonderful woman felt numb, she was so blocked up with suppressed rage and hopelessness. Her inner child was shunted aside and rejected. As she felt acceptable enough to express her uniqueness, she began for the first time to feel a sense of hope and empowerment awaken within her. She began to feel for the first time a sense of self-esteem and worthiness that allowed feelings of peace.

In the movie *Fried Green Tomatoes*, the main character feels ignored and unrecognized. She is overweight, filling her need for love with donuts and pastries. She tries in vain to get the attention she needs from her preoccupied husband, who's more interested in food and television. Finally, she focuses her attention on herself, giving herself the love she needs in the form of a healthy relationship, exercise, and work that reinforces her independence and self-esteem. She asserts her needs and values in her relationship with her husband. Through loving herself, she expresses self-esteem in creative work, honest interaction, and having the courage to be herself. Finally, she finds the love she has been seeking within her own self.

This is what it means to be a heroine!

As we honor our need to look within and find out who we are, our unique self becomes visible. As we reach within, seeking the help of a competent therapist if necessary, our healthy self-esteem no longer needs to rely on illness to gain the recognition and attention we require to live happy lives with a sense of inner peace.

In caring enough to give yourself the love you need to allow your inner child to become recognized or visible, you will find your whole world changing. As you stop trying to get the approval of others and learn to love yourself, others of like nature will be drawn to you and you will find yourself in the loving and nurturing relationships you had only heretofore dreamed of. This is how it works.

I would like to close this chapter with an excerpt from *The Ugly Duckling*, by Hans Christian Andersen.

As soon as they saw him, the swans began to swim toward him. "No doubt I am about to meet my end," thought the duckling, "but if I am to be killed, then rather by these beautiful creatures than by hunters, farm wives or long winters." And he bowed his head to await the blows.

But lo! In the reflection in the water he saw a swan in full dress: snowy plumage, sloe eyes and all. The ugly duckling at first did not recognize himself, for he looked just like the beautiful strangers, just like those he had admired from afar.

And it turned out that he was one of them after all. His egg had accidentally rolled into a family of ducks. He was a swan, a glorious swan. And for the first time, his own kind came near him and touched him gently and lovingly with their wing tips. They groomed him with their beaks and swam round and round him in greeting.

Exercise:

Take a piece of paper and write down some of the things you need to do in order to make your little child feel comforted and loved. How can you make your little child feel recognized and visible? Perhaps relationships with emotionally unavailable people are reinforcing your childhood patterns of feeling dis-appointed or unrecognized. Make the effort it takes to get in touch with the reality of your feelings about yourself and your life. And then ask for God's help in making the constructive changes necessary for self-esteem and inner peace. I have found that there is nothing to fear in facing the truth of our feelings. It is only denial and self-deception that keep us suffering and trapped within ourselves in hopelessness. Take that first step and free your unique self. Remember, the truth will set you free! You are worth it!

Affirmations:

- I love and accept myself exactly as I am, and I am taking care of me.

- I am good enough.

- I lovingly enfold the child that is myself with the white light of unconditional love.

7

*If you want truth as badly as a drowning man wants
air, you will realize it in a split second!*

—Upanishads

*The stone which the builders rejected
has become the cornerstone.*

—Psalm 118:22

Finding the Authentic Self: Opening to Receive Grace

Some months ago, I was riding in my car when I felt overwhelmed with a sense of joy and ecstasy. Such was the consciousness of my bliss that, for a moment, I wondered if I could go on driving in such a transported state of ecstasy. As I looked out the window, the sky, the clouds, the trees all looked and felt so divinely beautiful that I felt tears of pure joy spring to my eyes in gratitude for this moment of life. As I experienced this divine sense of bliss, I suddenly felt what seemed like water sprinkling on my hands and arms. This sensation travelled down through my legs and was so real that I thought perhaps it had started to rain and I had not noticed it coming through the window. I checked the sky for a cloudburst, but the sun was shining brightly. Then I wondered whether the air conditioner was leaking, and I checked that too. I realized then that this sensation of trickling water was being felt on my skin within my own self. Since it had accompanied the divine sense of ecstasy, I puzzled over the experience long after it had passed, and I asked God for information.

A few weeks later, I was reading a book about mystical experiences induced by the hallucinogenic drug, Adam. One of the participants of the experiment had experienced what she considered a state of grace. She described the experience of grace as a "spiritual washing."

I deeply identified with this explanation. Grace is something over which we do not have any control. The only thing we can do to invite grace into our lives in any way is to lead lives worthy of receiving grace. The great sage Krishnamurti puts it in very simple terms. He says that it is like keeping a room clean and tidy. You can sweep that room clean and fresh every day, but keeping the room clean is not going to open the window and let in the sunlight. The window is opened from the outside. However, if you make the consistent effort of caring enough and believing enough to live this way, keeping the room clean, then one day that window might just open. If it does, you will be ready by your thorough and persistent house cleaning to receive the sunlight.

The thorough and persistent housecleaning I am referring to is the inner work involved in the honest expression of feelings and the effort to understand who you are and to make the changes necessary each day to be a healthy, caring human being.

Living life in this manner causes us to feel good about ourselves, to enter into a state of humility, receptivity and trust—the essentials to be worthy of grace. If we do not cultivate the awareness to live in this manner, then we are too self-absorbed, fearful and guilty to invite amazing grace into our lives.

Grace is a gift from God. To open ourselves to grace, we must ask for it with all our heart, crying from our innermost being and turning to God for salvation. We must then *let go to God, and trust*.

Our free will as human beings gives us tremendous power. Such is God's great love for us that we are given at every moment the opportunity to exercise our power of choice. In living our lives exercising right speech, right action and right behavior, we make room in our lives to choose to receive the great miracle of grace, should God choose to bless us accordingly.

I remember quite clearly and precisely my experience of spontaneous healing. As I felt the powerful energy of light enter the top of my head and course through my body, my rational mind was in a total state of fear. My heart was beating wildly, and my rational mind was screaming, "Get up! Get up! Stop the experience! You're having a heart attack!"

At that moment, a point of awareness within me was able to see that these commands were part of an endless litany of fears, a never-ending tape of fear that was Not Who I Am. This point of awareness within me saw and heard the tape, but chose at that moment to let go to the powerful radiant energy flowing through my body. As I did so, as I see it now, I let go of fear and made a choice to receive love. The point of awareness that saw the tape and chose to let go to the love, is Who I Am. It is who each one of us is. It is the Authentic Self.

After the intensity of this experience, when I slumped over on the couch, I experienced for the first time in my life a state of total peace and well being. For the first time in my life, I had no thoughts, just a complete peace, which expressed itself as an inner knowing, a sweet smile within. This gentle, loving, all-knowing awareness was none other than my Self. In making the choice to let go of fear, I found the love I had been searching for all my life. In that moment of grace, the pain and tragedy of my life disintegrated into the ashes of illusion. All the suffering was an illusion! This Authentic Self was totally untouched by the pain of my life, and it manifested as total, unconditional love, joy and peace.

Though it took many years for this experience to flow through my being in full realization, I allowed it to change my life immediately. I saw that the rational mind would come in and try to rob me of the experience as it had done so often in my life.

This time, however, was different. I had the medical proof of my test results to scientifically confirm the experience.

What indeed had happened to me? What are spontaneous healings all about? How can a person have cancer, sometimes all through his or her body, and then, in one instant, be healed of illness? All these questions surfaced for me to answer.

My search for answers led me to volunteer at the hospital, to share my message of hope with the seriously ill. I learned so much through this experience. It took a lot of courage to confront my fears each morning as I went to work in the cancer ward. I'm so glad I conquered my resistance, because I was able to learn and experience so much from people suffering the illness of cancer that I was encouraged to begin my own practice, Self-Healing, where the people I worked with taught me even more!

While volunteering in the cancer ward, I encountered a pervasive atmosphere of despair that was almost palatable as soon as you entered the ward. This despair was evident not only in the patients, but in the doctors and nurses as well! So often nurses would take me aside and thank me for my cheerful and optimistic presence on the floor. One nurse confessed to me that she looked forward to the days I worked because the whole atmosphere of the ward changed. She thanked me for the gifts of love and hope I shared and thanked me for giving both patients and staff permission to hope!

The power of the attending physician became evident. I saw patients bloom with optimism upon encouragement from their doctor. I also saw people literally die immediately after being told there was no hope of survival. This showed me the tremendous power of belief in the healing of illness, the first step being the hope that healing is possible.

I made friends with more than one patient on the ward. One day, I entered the room of a man seriously ill, indeed "dying" of cancer. My heart went out to him as I saw the still, silent figure barely alive beneath the sheets, the face a mask of hopelessness and weary despair.

I warily approached his bed and said the first thing that entered my mind to help him. "Would you like some juice?" I offered. His eyes, far removed, looked up at me. I was surprised when he answered yes, so surprised that I stuttered, "Now?"

He almost smiled with cynicism as he immediately replied, "When, then?" Yes, indeed! No time like the present, especially when you're dying! His reply flustered me, and I rushed from the room to find him some pineapple juice, which was also my grandmother's favorite, and mine. In a way this old gentleman reminded me of my grandmother, with his compellingly aware reply.

I began to check up on him routinely, making him as comfortable as I could without intruding on his privacy. He seemed almost humorously grateful to me for my attention, but this was just a feeling he imparted to me, since he rarely spoke.

One morning, while dispensing from my cart of water and juice, I saw that his room was filled with people. As I looked closer, I saw a priest performing Last Rites over my friend. The cross and purple vestments of the priest were harsh and frightening realities. His bed was surrounded with friends and family on their knees crying and praying. I stood outside the door, crying, my heart beating fast. One of the nurses came over to me saying, "He's dying." I said a prayer for my friend, completed my duties, and went home.

A few days later, I returned to the hospital. I found myself avoiding his room and felt unprepared to see the freshly-made, empty bed that would convey the actual fact of my friend's death to me.

As I passed the room, I was shocked to see my friend sitting up on the edge of the bed, eating a hearty breakfast and joking with the nurses!

In nothing less than a state of shock, I shyly entered the room. He saw me immediately and boomed out, "Come in! No, it isn't a ghost, it's me! I'm alive!" I had never seen him more alive, peaceful, relaxed and happy. The cynicism and hopelessness were gone from his face and eyes. The nurses were bustling about his room, helping him to pack.

"I'm going home today," he told me softly and kindly.

"What happened?" I asked him.

He smiled. "I wasn't ready to die," he answered. "No, not me. I'm not going yet." Then he laughed.

His complete transformation reminded me of the change in Ebenezer Scrooge after the harrowing Christmas Eve experience of viewing his own tombstone with the Ghost of Christmas Future. In the morning, Old Scrooge was absolutely giddy with happiness, just for being alive.

The experience of my friend's dramatic and startling recovery showed me the power we have within ourselves to make choices that can dramatically alter our destinies. It showed me the tremendous power of the human mind and the human will.

We have resources within ourselves about which we know little or nothing, resources of strength that go unexplored and unexercised. This experience and others caused me to investigate some of the possible scientific explanations for the miracle that had happened to me.

A Course in Miracles states that just one moment free of fear is necessary for instantaneous healing. This of course is an explanation, but how does it happen?

As I probed this mystery, I uncovered information stating that the human body, upon molecular and atomical observation with the highest-powered equipment, is not "solid." Our bodies are composed of atoms separately and completely surrounded by light. Isn't this amazing? Light is part of who we are! Does it not make perfect sense, then, that in one given moment this light could be released in a flow throughout the body, changing the structure of the body itself?

This I found to be a possible explanation, as much as any miracle can be explained.

As we unblock from fear, resentment, and guilt, this healing light can then flow through our bodies, healing us.

A study of spontaneous remission of cancer by Dr. O. Carl Simonton revealed that all such patients, regardless of what they considered the cause of healing, had consistently held a positive idea that their healing was taking or had taken place.

Dr. Simonton also states that before the disease of AIDS was labelled incurable by the media, he was able to help people heal of the illness. After a mass belief system developed that AIDS was incurable, people stopped *believing* that healing was possible. Now, however, fortunately, the tide is reversing once again as books such as *Why I Survive AIDS*, by Niro Asistent, are assimilated into the belief system of our society.

Such is the tremendous power of belief!

One of the most fascinating and moving documentaries I have ever seen was an interview with some of the survivors of the "miracle of the Andes" from the movie, *Alive*. These people overcame unspeakable tragedy, heartbreak and adversity to survive in seemingly impossible circumstances. Wearing only plastic bags to cover their feet, two of the survivors heroically challenged the Andes to find freedom in Peru, thus rescuing their companions, who remained stranded in the mountains. One of the true heroes of the story, Nando, stated that he *believed it was possible.*

Was it not Jesus who said, "As ye believe, so shall it be"?

Sometimes remembering a childhood experience of belief can trigger your faith as an adult.

I remember as a small child, going to the movies with my brothers. We were brimming over with excitement to see *20,000 Leagues Under the Sea.* When we arrived at the theater, we did not have enough money for all of us to go in.

On the way home, I fiercely prayed to God for help. God heard the innocent child's prayer and responded. As the three of us were crossing the highway to start on our way, I noticed a $5 bill blowing against the grass in the wind. I snatched it up with my brothers' shouts of joy surrounding me. I was a hero!

This childhood memory of the power of prayer was revealed to me in my fight for my life through cancer. Perhaps you too can unearth a childhood experience of magic and belief that will assist you as an adult in *healing and believing.*

There was an episode of the TV series *Twilight Zone* I will always remember.

To me, through its enchanting mysticism, it illustrates perfectly the chance opportunities life gives us to exercise our power of belief.

The opening scene begins in a nursing home in Florida, where the old people have become bored, bitter and cynical. Enter a strange, dynamic drifter whose magical presence begins to stimulate hope in the cynical residents.

Soon the atmosphere of the nursing home is changing. People are having fun! The spirit of love and adventure is being awakened in their hearts.

However, there is a group who oppose the changes and wish to remain hard and bitter. Their cynicism prevents them from opening to love.

Soon the spirited group led by the magical mentor hatches up a plan: at midnight they will all sneak out of the nursing home and play their childhood game of "Kick the Can."

At midnight, giggling like children, they begin their exodus from the nursing home.

It is a brisk autumn evening, clear and sparkling with a full moon to light the way.

As the dry leaves scuttle in the wind, the beautiful older people begin their magical game.

The other residents stay behind, awakening the authorities about the others who have "gone crazy," and are "breaking the rules."

As the cynics and authorities rush out into the night to restrain the players, beneath the light of a street lamp they are amazed to find a group of laughing, shouting children playing Kick the Can.

The excited children turn to wave good-bye to the others before vanishing into the night.

The cynics in vain try to reach out, crying, "Wait for us!"

But the moment is lost, the chance opportunity dissolving before their eyes, as the now-rejuvenated children flee into the mystery.

Don't be afraid to take the risk and believe. Come out of the bleachers, onto the playing field and live!

What strange and mysterious creatures we are! How interesting we are, and what mysteries there are to explore and probe within ourselves!

Recently, I was at an airport waiting for my plane, which had been delayed for two hours. Airports can be the scene of much awareness and spiritual revelation and, that day, as I watched the thousands and thousands of people who, irritated and bored, glanced repeatedly at their watches, while thousands of others rushed here, there and everywhere, a thought suddenly occurred to me:

"No one here knows how they got to this earth or where they are going when they leave, yet no one takes the time to slow down enough to find out!"

Who we are is just not important! This great mystery of life is going on at every moment, but for most people this incredible adventure goes unexplored until a crisis brings it momentarily to light.

As I was reeling from this great awareness, I suddenly became hungry for shrimp cocktail. Ah! The ever-present humanness; we cannot escape it and must honor it.

So I got up from my seat in the clogged waiting room, leaving it for ten others to dive toward. I left them wrestling with each other as I headed toward a seafood restaurant. I sat down and ordered the shrimp cocktail. As I did so, I noticed a man at the next table looking over at me as if he were going to approach me and, sure enough, he did!

As I ate my shrimp cocktail, he told me that his mother was seriously ill with cancer. His father and brother had committed suicide. He was a successful attorney who was desperately unhappy inside himself and wanted to believe that life had meaning and purpose. His eyes were filled with tears as he spoke his truth and listened to my reply. As I said, airports are great places for spiritual revelations, as people know they will in all likelihood never see each other again.

I told him about my work and gave him helpful information that he needed, plus the names of some books he could read to further explore his questions. We talked until our respective planes had arrived and it was time for us to depart. We shook hands as friends. I knew the information I gave him could divert the course of his life if he allowed it to. I believe that it did and that he is happier now with more of a grasp on things. I choose to believe this.

The point I am making is that at any moment we can choose to overcome the barriers that separate us as human beings and to reach out in a higher order of action and behavior. Perhaps the answers are present within that person who just crossed your path; who knows?

I still recall with gratitude the police officer who stopped me for speeding while I was on my way to my radiation treatments during my first bout with cancer. When he found out the reason for my haste—mainly that I was late for my treatment—he personally escorted me at a rip-roaring 80 mph for one and a half hours to the hospital.

My mother taught me never to talk to strangers, but the way I feel about it now is this: we are all human beings, we are in this together, and the help we need is usually right at hand if we have the awareness to follow our intuition and reach out for it.

Keep your eyes open in awareness. Tear down the barriers that separate us as human beings, and then move forward into the flow of life. To do this, many times you must "talk to strangers."

"The Grace of God is in every shape around." This is a quote from *Daughter of Fire,* the diary of Irina Tweedie's spiritual training with a Sufi master.

The first time I had cancer, I wrote in my journal that finding out what love was, meant more to me than "my next breath of air."

There is a quote from the ancient Indian scriptures, the *Upanishads,* that states, "If you want truth as badly as a drowning man needs air, you will realize it in a split second." These words are realized truth for me.

How badly do you want to live? What risks and measures are you willing to take to find out what life is all about? Or are you like the thousands of people at the airport, rushing here, there and everywhere without a moment to slow down and reflect upon the meaning of life? Who are You?

Especially for those who face serious illness, these questions have tremendous import. I have found that God will help in every aspect of our lives, if we believe this and allow it.

A story told by a Sufi master reveals this truth. There was a man who travelled to India in search of a saint. He was told that the saint would be at a certain funeral at a given time, and that he could be spotted by the circle of gold above his head.

The man went to the funeral and saw that each person there had a halo of gold around his head. However, as the people filed away, only one man remained with the golden halo. This was the saint. When the man questioned the Sufi master about this, he was told that the circle of gold represented a person's spiritual awareness of the presence of God. At funerals, all people open to this awareness momentarily. However it is only the truly spiritual person who keeps that awareness of God, who lives it and feels it in the everyday activities of life.

It is this awareness of the presence of God that sets the hero, the spiritual adventurer, apart from the throngs of unaware multitudes, preoccupied in the mundane activities of everyday life.

Each one of us has the capacity to be in what Joseph Campbell terms "God's Country" at each moment, even at airports.

One night I had a dream. I dreamed that I was driving a bus full of people to the top of a mountain. There was a hook-and-ladder fire engine blocking the ascent. From out of nowhere came a woman named Grace, dressed in white robes, who unblocked the path to the top of the mountain.

When I woke up, I realized the meaning of the dream and felt the beauty and faith of it. Later on, however, in the course of my day, I forgot the dream.

After I had finished up at the office for the day, I did something I rarely did at that time. I drove over to a little shop where I had seen an outfit in the window that had appealed to me a few weeks before. I entered the shop in haste and tried on the outfit. I liked it and was making out the check for the garment when I asked the salesclerk, "Who do I make this check out to? What is the name of the shop?"

"J. Grace," she replied.

A shock of awareness went through me as I remembered my dream. I laughed outloud and told her of my dream. I later wrote it down on a piece of paper. It was evident God wanted me to remember it. Once again the Beloved was winking his eye at me, saying, "I am with you," perhaps so that I could tell it to you, so that it can have meaning for you.

It has been my experience that not much is written about grace. However, I feel as if I could talk on and on about it, because it has become such an essential part of my life experience. It was only through God's grace that the tragedy and pain of my life was transformed into love, joy, peace and health. What a thrilling statement of hope that is!

Follow Your Bliss

When we are not being true to ourselves, deep within our hearts we have the feeling that, no matter how hard we try, we are not real people. We are fraudulent. We feel this way because we are not authentic in our feelings or actions.

We stay in relationships that are stale and dry because we are afraid to move forward into the unknown; we work at jobs we despise for money or gain, or the fear that we are not capable of better.

We live this way because we do not trust ourselves or the universe to provide us with the opportunities we need to grow and change.

I firmly know and believe that if you do what you love, the money will follow. If you believe this as well, it will be true for you.

I also believe that as we become restless within relationship, it is time to grow and change within ourselves within that relationship, or we must have the faith it takes to let go of the relationship and make room for change. If we act correctly, in accordance with our inner guidance, the universe will provide us with the prosperity and the relationships that allow us to be joyful and alive each day. Remember, if we live life correctly, we always move toward a higher livelihood, a higher purpose, a higher love.

But how can all this be possible for you if you don't believe it?

I feel that God and the angels must mourn the fact that human beings feel too guilty, fearful and unworthy to receive their higher good. We must move forward to do this.

Don't wait until tomorrow to begin to create the changes necessary to improve your life.

True change means opening to creation. Get in touch with your creativity and allow the light to enter and heal.

Look back in time to childhood and remember the things you loved to do that charmed and delighted you. Why must you leave those things behind in order to grow up? We must learn how to play and enjoy as feeling adults, pouring our energy into actions that allow us to feel good about who we are.

Your creativity will feel good to your body. The flow of creation will pour into your life and turn the tide to love and inner healing.

Take your life in your hands and create! Get in touch with a cherished dream and believe it can come true. Then make it come true! Come out of hiding so others can see you. You are beautiful and powerful! Have you forgotten?

Meditation: Fountain of Healing Waters

Feel yourself relaxing. Close your eyes, going deeply within to a source of unconditional love and peace. . . . Feel yourself opening, opening to receive the light and beauty of divine love and healing. . . .

As your eyes relax, journey without fear in the warm darkness. Perhaps you are aware of swirling colors of purple or red. Feel the comfort of this inner space. . . .

As you quietly journey further, you can visualize a light within. . . . Feel yourself responding, flowing inward towards the light. . . . As you emerge from the darkness, you are literally bathed in a brilliant white light. All here is light and radiance. Within the comfort here you can visualize a fountain. . . . The sparkling pure waters of this fountain are alive with love and healing. . . .

There is a cup near the fountain. . . . Go to it and fill your cup to the brim with the healing waters of the fountain. Drink of the purity, the serenity of the crystal water. . . . Feel the miraculous waters replenish and renew your spirit. Drink easily and feel yourself refreshed, healed and renewed. . . .

Rest here. You may partake of this inner fountain any time you wish. . . . It is eternally available to you. Take a moment to experience a sensation of bliss and divine love. . . . Nothing can disturb the calm peace of your soul. All is well here. . . .

Feel the divine love and healing. . . . Freely fill your cup at any moment you choose. . . . There is respite here; comfort and peace. . . .

As you return to consciousness, tap into the love and healing you have experienced here. . . . Let it be part of your day. Slow down and remember your spiritual nature in the course of your day. . . . Relax, have fun, be in balance within yourself this day.

Affirmations:

꘎ I am opening to receive the gifts of love that are here for me.

- I am opening to receive God.

- I am worthy to receive the grace of God.

- I let go of the misery of the past.

- I let go of my belief that life cannot be wonderful and joy-ful.

- I realize this is a false belief based on the painful experiences of childhood.

- I open to the belief that life is wonderful and good, and I am ready and open to receive my good.

- I am grateful for my many blessings. I am grateful to the wonderful helpers on my path who gave me and continue to give me unconditional love.

- I now receive this love with gratitude and joy.

- I am free to live a joyful life.

- I am free to be who I am.

I WANDERED LONELY AS A CLOUD
William Wordsworth

I wandered lonely as a cloud that floats on high o'er vale and hill
When all at once I spied a crowd
A host of golden daffodils
Above the lake
Between the trees
Fluttering and dancing in the breeze

. . . . .

When oft upon my couch
I lie in vacant or in pensive mood
They flash upon my inward eye
Which is the bliss of solitude
And then my heart with pleasure fills
And dances with the daffodils

8

*"Well, now that we have seen each other," said the
Unicorn, "if you believe in me, I'll believe in you.
Is that a bargain?"*

—LEWIS CARROLL, *Through the Looking Glass*

*The clearest way into the Universe is
through a forest wilderness.*

—JOHN MUIR, "John of the Mountains"

Sacred Affirmations of Nature

To guide us on our path in life, we are given affirmations.
Affirmations are, literally, statements of faith. In order to recognize these affirmations, one must have a simple, innocent
mind. One must be in awareness.

If we are constantly in thought, trying to figure out our lives,
we live as in a delusion, apart from the flow of life.

How can thought, which is dead, figure out life, a constant
flowing force?

We must turn to life itself, to reality, to guide us along our
path. After reaching inward through prayer and asking God to
fill our needs, we must then turn outward in order to see the
manifestations of guidance, or grace.

These outward manifestations of guidance are given in the
simplest, most beautiful ways and forms, many times through
and in nature. In nature we find the utter beauty, simplicity and
sweetness of divine love and guidance.

How utterly simple, mysterious, numerous and innocent are the affirmations of God.

When we cry out sincerely from the heart for help and guidance, we release our expectations, then literally open our eyes, so that we may see clearly with innocence. Only then may we receive the ecstatic experience of oneness, divine love and healing that is the awareness of an *answer*—for that is what an affirmation is—an *answer* to a prayer in the simplest of forms.

In order to receive this sacred answer, we must have faith, believe, and open our eyes in innocence and awareness.

Only then does the Beloved wink his eye at us in sacred affirmation.

In the course of my life, I have been blessed with answers in the rarest, deepest ways imaginable. These answers or affirmations spoke to me on a profoundly personal level and evoked an inner response that can only be called Truth. This response was felt at the core of my being and had nothing to do with my intellectual mind.

An affirmation strikes a deep inner chord that is mystical, deeply personal, magical and ecstatic. It is the total awareness of Being, or God. Our total Being resonates in oneness with all creation. Instead of being lost, in one moment we are rescued, found, loved, praised and encouraged to go forth in rightness. We are cheered on in the sweetest, most joyous realms of child-like wonder and innocence.

Indeed, an affirmation is a return to innocence. It is a delight and a surprise.

Who can remember the childhood feeling of crickets chirping in the stillness of a summer evening, of a shimmering full moon, of the skies casting long shadows in the pearly whiteness of night, of fireflies winking in the darkness? Who can remember a feeling of comfort and safety, the peace and serenity found in oneness with nature, the thrilling ebb and flow of the cosmic heartbeat?

"Be Still and Love"

There is a mystery in the heart of all living things, a sacred mystery.

Long ago, when I lived in Canada, in moments of intense emotional suffering, I would leave my cabin and embark on a walk through the forest, seeking solace in nature.

Each wildflower that colorfully grew along my path smiled to greet me as I walked; the white violet exuded its exquisite perfume just for me. A wet autumn leaf on a rock reminded me of something. The emerald moss afforded a comforting chair.

As I prayed, suffering in solitary loneliness, a bluejay lit on a branch to soothe the pain; two ladybugs crawling on a stone cheered my heavy heart.

One day, I found myself seated on a large rock next to an old maple tree. So deep in suffering was I, turning my eyes toward the tree for an answer. I looked at this glorious maple tree, at the gorgeous heavy trunk that led up to leafy arms strewn with turning autumn leaves of stunning colors—gold, orange and red. Its branches were literally alive with dozens of chirping birds, charming varieties that swooped and dived joyfully within its leafy arms. This tree had to be the most glorious in the forest, I thought—so alive, ancient, beautiful and serene. Its presence exuded strength.

I turned to the tree in my sorrow and pressed my forehead against its firm, supportive trunk.

"What can you tell me?" I asked it aloud. "What answer do you have for me?"

"Be still and love," the tree replied.

I felt myself become calm. As I opened my eyes, I noticed that my head had been bent on a portion of bark that seemed to swell in a healthy ring around the tree's circumference.

As I studied the ring, I saw that beneath it was wound, in circles, several strands of barbed wire, the sort one finds dividing property lines in the country.

I felt for the tree! How it must have suffered, being twisted round with barbed wire! And yet, it had healed itself, fortifying itself to heal the wound. Its roots pressed deep into the rich soil of the forest; its branches stretched upward towards heaven, alive with cheerful birds!

Surely if this tree could heal itself, then so could I!

I allowed my heart to soar in gladness for the wonderful tree. It held a powerful truth for me, a message of spirit.

"Be still and love," I said aloud. I pressed my back against the tree and felt its strength flow into me. With gratitude, I let go of my suffering and said a prayer of thanks to the wondrous tree. Thus, for the moment, I felt the blessing of inner peace. I carry that blessing in my heart to this day.

Isn't that a wonderful story? Why are we losing contact with our trees, our forests? Why are we losing the humility, simplicity and innocence to respectfully connect with nature, with this planet that houses our very being?

I think that in our quest for material possessions we have forgotten how to live. We have forgotten how to love. We have forgotten the importance of the awareness of love and the experiences that truly make us happy.

When I lived in the woods, I felt a oneness with all of creation. I looked to nature for wisdom, and nature revealed her secrets to me.

REQUEST
Angela Passidomo Trafford

When I die
Bury me on the hill
Under the spruces
Near my favorite rock

My friends are here
In the blue and green glade

Reaching out leafy arms
Offering the solace of plant and soil

Look—over there
Is the nest of branches I made
And here the maple I climbed
To confer with the chickadees

Here, where the trees
Are my professors
The changing sky my lamp
The earth my mother and friend

Bury me here
And let my body
Become one
With my friends and family
Please
Do not take me to another hill
To lie with strangers
Who would never know me

My Father
Whispered to me
And calmed my troubled spirit
Saying I will know peace
One day
After the battles
Here

The Mansion in the Long Grass

One day, I received a letter from my mother saying that my brother had just purchased a beautiful mansion. After I read the letter, I took a walk in the woods and came across a small field of wildflowers. It was springtime, and the tall grass was filled with purple cow vetch, black-eyed susans and white daisies.

I dropped down in the long grass and pressed my face among the flowers. I could feel the warm sun on the back of my neck and smell the freshness of the air and grass. I opened my eyes and spotted a beetle crawling up a stalk of timothy, its black-shell body gleamed blue-green iridescence in the sunlight. A bottle-green fly landed close by, the color of emeralds.

I breathed deeply and experienced a moment of pure beauty and ecstasy.

"Oh mother!" I said aloud, "I wish you could see *this* beautiful mansion!"

In such a sparkling moment of awareness, all is well in the world.

What the Sky Told Me: The Great Secret

One summer afternoon, while sitting on the porch of my cabin, I took out a mirror and looked into it. Who was I? "Who are you?" I asked myself. The face stared back at me with questioning eyes. "Who are you?" I asked again. A tormented expression stared back at me seeming to say, "And who are *you?*"

I threw the mirror down and cried. I was in an abusive marriage; I had lost my identity. I didn't know who I was anymore.

I wept bitter tears, asking God for help.

While sitting on the log steps, I raised my eyes to the summer sky. It was an incredible blue, with fluffy white clouds drifting in the blueness.

I riveted my attention on the sky. I felt a great secret about to be revealed to me.

I strained my being to experience the "great secret," beseeching God for answers in my deep sorrow.

All at once, I knew. In one mystical moment I experienced the answer.

"Take care of yourself," came the reply.

I never forgot that response, the great secret: **Take care of yourself.**

It took me a lifetime to learn how.

I am aware as I write this, that these affirmations seem like fairy tales. In fact, that *is* what an affirmation feels like as it is happening. It feels like everything you thought life could be, everything you ever dreamed of is coming true. I guess it is like the song that Frank Sinatra sings:

> "Fairy Tales can come true, it can happen to you,
> If you're young at heart. . . ."

Being young at heart is the key: "Lest ye like little children be, ye cannot know the Kingdom of Heaven," said all-knowing Jesus.

So, please, if you have been made cynical and hard by the passage of time, tragedy, and circumstances, shed the cynicism of life and embark with me on this adventure.

Be like little children again and share with me some magical moments of grace and affirmation.

The Spider in the Snow

One winter day, I stoked the fire in the wood stove and watched as the fire leaped from the burning embers.

I was lonely and despondent. I stared out the cabin window at the falling snow. It was a blizzard, and I could hear the wind wailing as the snowflakes swirled and the cabin logs creaked in the storm.

I was alone, though another was in the house. Have you ever felt that way? It is the worst loneliness.

I threw my old fur coat on, pulled on my boots, and opened the door.

In my suffering, all I could think of was escape.

I felt relief as I walked along, my footprints tracking a path through the falling snow. The pointed spruces looked dark green and splendid against the earth and sky as I worked my way up the hill into the woods.

The snowflakes lashed my face. It was freezing cold and the snow had piled high. I was up to my knees in drifts, but still I propelled myself onward; the woods and snow held only welcome for me, such was my suffering within that cabin.

I pressed against the snow and felt the violence of the wind. Mindlessly, I walked farther, praying silently to myself, not knowing where I was going or why.

As I reached the top of the hill, at a fork in the road, I could feel the fury of the storm. I could hardly catch my breath as the wind beat against my face and the snowflakes blinded my eyes.

All of a sudden, the wind and snow *stopped*, and it was calm. The sun appeared and warmed my face as just a few flakes drifted through the air.

I looked down. I was up to my waist in snow. My fur coat trailed around me like a cape.

I looked in front of me and gasped. I could hardly believe my eyes. I felt the sense of a separate reality.

A small spider was walking toward me on top of the snow. I bent closer to look.

The spider crept slowly, leaving a luminous trail as it walked. Even the spider itself was luminous.

I caught my breath, experiencing the enormity of the moment, the incredible spectacle I was witnessing. It was impossible that this was happening; a spider could never survive this.

I felt I could actually look into the eyes of the luminous spider and feel its awareness. It needed help. I felt all time suspend as I reached forth my hand. At that same instant, the wind picked up and I was hit with the full fury of the storm, once again.

I looked around me and felt the awesomeness of Nature, of God, of myself, of all living things.

I made my way back to the cabin in a state of wonder, almost unaware of my body or the storm.

I pulled open the door of the cabin and went inside. My hair, coat, clothing, were soaking wet. My face, hands and legs were beet red and numb with the cold.

I put on a pair of velvet pants and a soft, flowing top. The fabrics felt comforting and loving to my body. I ran my hands over my skin and felt the wonder of my body. Tears filled my eyes. I was ALIVE. It was a gift. I hugged myself in a moment of love and reverence. I was unaccustomed to honoring such feelings. I sat by the wood stove warming myself in total peace.

What an awesome mystery this world is! How little we know or understand about it, yet we take for granted each precious moment of our lives and our relationships with people and nature.

We must slow down enough for nature and for life itself to lend richness and meaning to our lives.

How intensely glorious one moment can be if we are there—fully, emotionally present—instead of caught, like hamsters on a wheel, in our thinking minds.

Finding the Source of Thought

Why are we stuck up in thought all the time?

One day in late summer I decided to find out where thought came from. I wanted to experience the source of all thought.

I walked through the woods, enjoying the nurturing presence of the trees and flowers. I reached a small field of wheat-colored grass and lay down to rest. In the silence, I closed my eyes, turning inward in meditation. Thoughts, like little slippery creatures, slithered through my consciousness faster than I could fathom. I relaxed further into Being.

A gentle breeze wafted across my thighs—a memory registered. Another light gust of wind caressed my arms—instantly
a memory registered as thought.

I thereby concluded that memories were trapped in intricate
nets of awareness throughout the body. As each awareness was
stimulated by an outside force, thought was manifested.

Why do we then hook into thought, endlessly chewing
away, instead of being as a hollow bamboo reed, through which
the life force may freely pass in its constant ebb and flow?

Only in this manner may we truly experience *Being*.

All attempts to hold onto thought are manifestations of
resistance! Fear, anger, guilt and so on, all keep us endlessly
chained and imprisoned.

To experience true freedom as human beings, we must let
go of thought, overcoming our resistance to life itself.

Only then can we experience the miracles.

The Story of the Yellow Bird

A woman came to me for help in changing her life. She was
married to an alcoholic and had been trapped by guilt for many
years.

She was a fine person. Through our work together she
released the guilt. Her self-esteem grew to the point where she
made the decision to divorce her husband, who was not receptive to help or growth, and she went forward into the hope of a
better life.

She experienced the pain of loss with courage and fortitude,
giving herself the love and support necessary for growth and
change. As time passed, she shed her sadness and guilt, changed
her style of dress and became a curious, buoyant human being.

She fell in love and remarried and, at a turning point in her
inner work, decided her balance was such that she could devote
her full attention to her personal life.

I regarded her highly as a person and hoped she would return to uncover some basic issues that had begun to surface in our sessions together.

She attended the "Art of Living" workshop with Dr. Bernie Seigel and myself, and afterwards she phoned me to say that some disturbing thoughts and feelings had surfaced during a meditation on healing the Inner Child.

She felt she needed to resume our work together but was frightened and resistant. I reassured her that there was nothing to fear in the truth, that the truth would set her free.

In the course of our work together, this woman had consistently drawn birds in many of the pictures that we used to unearth unconscious feelings and messages. It was obvious that birds were messengers of truth for her. We often commented upon this mystery.

Our work began to uncover signals of sexual abuse in this woman's childhood; however, her fear of trusting her own recollections and perceptions blocked her from remembering. I commented that I believed much truth and information would come to her in dreams.

One afternoon, she started off our session by relating an incident that had happened to her that same morning. One of her co-workers had brought to her a small yellow bird that had apparently stunned itself by flying against the window in her office. The bird was injured, and some blood showed around its head. We commented on the rarity of the incident; small yellow birds of that nature are not native to the Naples, Florida area.

She had simulated a nest for the bird made of shredded paper, leaving a small space for it to see, while giving it protection as well. She placed the still, small body into the nest, hoping for its recovery.

As we began our work that day, she related a dream that she had had that week. She related it in an offhand way, as if it had not had much significance; however, a strong inner feeling suggested some great importance.

The dream related issues of sexual abuse with her brother.

She seemed uncomfortable, stating that she had no idea whether or not the dream had any truth to it. She remembered one small incident, but was unable to recall anything else. Since having the dream, she had manifested stomach cramps and a tightness in her chest, throat and midsection.

I asked her to draw me a picture of herself and her brother. She laughed uncomfortably and said, "What time, then or now?"

I replied, "Whatever time you wish. Anything that flows forth from you will be right and appropriate."

I turned on a tape of peaceful music and left her to create for a few minutes.

When I returned, she handed me the picture, laughing. I have found that many times inappropriate laughter accompanies revelations of sexual abuse. The laughter is a sign of truth to me of what the person is perceiving. It is a deflection of the shame and embarrassment that accompany the experience.

I perused the drawing carefully and was shocked at the truth of it. The drawing showed a little girl, with glasses; however, the glasses looked like a mask. The little girl was pointing an admonishing finger at her brother, a teenager. The brother pointed at her with one hand and had an expression of angry command or domination on his face. The other hand was on his genital area, which almost appeared as if the head of a penis was exposed.

In the right-hand corner of the picture, she had drawn, astonishingly enough, a bird cage, out of which was flying a yellow bird!

My client was unaware of the reality of what she had drawn, or of the importance.

When she was able to really "see" it, she gasped, totally taken aback.

In the course of the session, as she felt more assured of my love and concern for her, she began to unearth memories of repressed sexual abuse.

As a child of three, four and five, her brother would punish her for disobedience by forcing her to perform sexual acts for him.

As one such incident occurred, she remembered a yellow bird they had had in a cage, flying through the door of the cage, escaping!

Her body's messages revealed the guilt, anger, and shame of the experience enmeshed in awareness within her stomach, chest, and throat.

She expressed to me the guilt she felt at revealing these "secrets." She could no longer doubt the truth of her experience.

The guilt came up to be explored and released, and she was intensely motivated to further uncover and examine the truth of her childhood experiences. Her self-esteem increased as she gave herself the love and support she needed on her inner journey.

Together we thanked God and the Universe for sending her the message in the little yellow bird. We shared a moment of tears and gratitude at the awesome mystery of life, and for the sacred affirmation that supplied her with the help and encouragement she needed to find her inner truth.

A half hour after leaving the session in a total state of wonder, she called to say that the yellow bird had recovered, flown from the nest and was free!

Slow down and take the time to regain your innocence. Release the anger and hatred, and feel the freedom fill your heart making it light and joyous. Fill your being with unconditional love for who you are, and tap into the awesome mystery of life itself.

I have a deep and reverent feeling toward nature and all its marvelous creatures and could continue relating to you the secrets revealed to me through my love and reverence for nature, this planet and its creatures, all living things.

I will conclude this chapter by sharing with you one other magical experience, one of the most beautiful, humorous, sweet and innocent affirmations I have ever received or experienced.

The Crab and the Flower

One beautiful morning in Naples, I decided to absorb the beauty of nature by sitting out on a small pier on the water, just in back of my home.

It was my custom to do this, as I enjoy the peaceful feeling of the water and the many sea creatures that I can observe while sitting out on the pier relaxing.

As I walked toward the pier I saw the usual black crabs scuttle for safety at my approach. These little crabs were scavengers that lived around the pier. If one observes from a distance, it is interesting to watch them moving sideways across the boards intent on their business. However, they are exceedingly timid and scatter immediately at the sight of a human being, sometimes actually dropping and leaping off the pier into the water in their haste to escape.

So this morning I watched amused as the myriad of little creatures quickly disappeared when I sat down on the pier. I dangled my legs over the edge and took a deep breath of nature as I relaxed. I felt troubled this particular morning and closed my eyes in prayer.

I asked God to reveal his presence in my life and work. At this time I had been in this work for four years and there was no doubt at all that my prayers would be answered. It was just a matter of where, when and how. I even chuckled to myself, as I was aware of the sweet and touching manifestations of God, and wondered what would happen next.

I was not prepared, however, at the instant manifestation I received. (One is never prepared.) From across the pier I viewed a pair of eyes on stalks just peeking above the pier, observing me. I stared at the eyes. It was a curious sight, two eyes on stalks shyly regarding me. I was somewhat surprised as the eyes shifted upward and the body of the crab lifted itself slowly up onto the boards of the pier, so that the crab was level with myself.

Now my attention was definitely captured. This was a rare occurrence. I watched, captivated, as the crab slowly and carefully made its way toward me on the pier. I dared not move as I stared into its eyes—I knew it was overcoming tremendous fear to approach me.

My rational mind intervened saying, "Is it going to head straight toward me?" Yes! Yes it was! And here it came, in slow, deliberate steps, its eyes trustingly regarding mine.

I could not take my eyes off it in the timeless moments it took for the entire event to transpire, but as it came closer, I saw that its arm was upraised, and it was holding something in its claw.

I saw it held a tiny white flower aloft in its tiny black claw.

As it reached me in full realization of the miracle, I looked straight into its eyes, and I exclaimed aloud, "Is that for me?"

Whereupon the sweet, delightful little creature dropped the blossom on the board at my side and hurriedly scuttled away.

I wonderingly picked up the flower and turned my head to see those little eyes on stalks just peeking above the boards, apparently wanting to observe my reaction. I will never forget the timelessness of those moments, or the awareness and intelligence of that darling little crab.

"Oh, *thank you*!" I cried in gratitude and wonder. "Thank you, God, thank you!"

Please do stop and take the time to regard the wondrous creatures of this earth with reverence and respect—the lush flowering plants, the stately trees, the lizards hopping and leaping across your path. Slow down a moment to listen and watch the answers to your prayers unfold before your eyes. How will we find God in the sacred affirmations of nature if we do not have love and respect for the being that houses and protects us?

I promise you that if you care enough to open your eyes and look around you, you have a miracle in store for you, if you believe it. Celebrate your path in life.

Who could write of the beauty of nature without mentioning the American Indian, whose tradition includes a true spiritual reverence and respect for the earth and its creatures.

When I lived in the woods, nature sensed my love and reverence and responded to me with trust. Butterflies would light on my finger; the wild chickadees would rest on my hand as I brought out food to serve them. Once a doe and two fawn sipped water from the brook as I sat quietly beneath an apple tree. Moments such as these are sacred and unforgettable.

Be open and receptive to the wondrous healing gifts of nature, of God and the Universe. Open your eyes and ears to the beauty that surrounds you. Wake up and live, before it is too late! Read the book, *The Secret Garden*. Get in touch with nature as Mother and Healer.

The bounty and abundance you will receive will light your path in life and instill in your heart the sacredness of all living things.

I HAVE HOPE
Angela Passidomo Trafford

I have hope
As I sit here
In my favorite chair
A living plant
Flowing with grace and green
At my side
The open door
Emitting the cool air
And smells of spring

Fresh laundry snapping
In the sun, blazing white
All the sounds of
Everyday life clicking by
A squeaking bicycle
Reminding me
That I can still
Ache with gratitude
For just being alive
Just being loved
Just being lucky
Enough to be here
Today
Right now
Hope still alive
Like a smile
In my heart
Hope
That it all
Somehow
Will turn out right

God's Child
First and foremost
Woman
Wife and Mother

All my roles
As an earth child
Playing my part
The part
I chose
Somehow
Somewhere
Long ago

Not an easy one
To be sure
But still
It's all led to
This moment
This ecstasy

The smell of spring air
Wafting through the door
On gentle heavenly fingers
Touching my healthy skin

The sweet chirping
Of birds
Who feel
As I do
Who sing back to me
In joyous voices

I have hope!
I am alive!

Exercise

On a piece of paper, write down a "problem" you are seeking to find answers for in your life.

Now go outdoors and take a walk in nature. Be aware of the Beauty that surrounds you. Slow down. Observe the solution or help you need in a message from the abundance of nature and its living creatures.

Return to your abode and re-read the problem you had written down. How did your walk in nature heal and help you? What did you learn that you can apply in the healing of your life? Write the answer in your journal.

Affirmations:

🍂 I allow the joy and innocence of the natural world to flow through my being, healing me.

🍂 I feel the mystery and enchantment of the nature spirits and my animal friends, as a source of inner peace and wonder.

🍂 I give thanks to the Earth, my mother and friend.

🍂 My connection with the plants, insects and animals of this beautiful world fortifies my soul and gives me hope.

🍂 I see and feel the presence of God in all living things.

🍂 I feel the hum and throb of the Earth's heartbeat as a cosmic healing energy.

🍂 This reverence makes me whole and free.

🍂 I am one with the divine Creator. I am free.

UNLOCKING THE DOOR
Angela Passidomo Trafford

She lay back
Her face in heavenly repose
Revealing secrets
That would
Shatter the glass dome
Under which she had lived
As an innocent earth child

After the terror passed
She gathered the splintered shards
And planted them
In a garden she watered
With light and love and tears
Watching them grow
Emitting prisms and rainbows
And shafts of blazing brilliance
That promised
All she had ever dreamed of
All she had hoped for and
More

The new crystals
Could grow into shimmering towers
And sacred palaces

It all depended on her vision
And her power
And the strength of
A gardener's love

9

Wynken, Blynken and Nod one night
Sailed off in a wooden shoe—
Sailed on a river of crystal light
Into a sea of dew—

EUGENE FIELD, Wynken, Blynken and Nod

Vision is the art of seeing things invisible.

JONATHAN SWIFT

We are not hypocrites in our sleep.

WILLIAM HAZLITT

The Secret World of Dreams

Deep within us lies a land uncharted and yet fathomable. In dreaming we reach a world where we meet—ourselves!

Dreams are messages from the unconscious mind. In learning to decipher dreams we receive valuable information that we can use to guide us on our path in life.

A dream is a puzzle and a mystery. It is a key to learning more about who we are, about where our true feelings lie and, in some cases, about other lives or realms. A dream can be a clarion of prophecy.

In learning to interpret our dreams, we delve into the exploration of our being, diving into aspects of ourselves that lead to a deeper understanding of who we are, of what we truly feel and our innermost longings and desires. A dream is the hidden reality of who we are.

In many cases a dream is a journey into mystical, psychic revelations. In reading the symbols and hieroglyphics of dreams we may better chart our course in life on this earth. As a navigator uses the stars to steer his course, so the dreamer may incorporate the information received in dreams to better understand and discover the choices that enrich and create his or her life.

The dreamer may look to dreams as the vast inner space to find answers to his deepest, most intimate questions in the quest for personal happiness, love and inner peace.

Dreams are the gateway to the unconscious. In passing courageously through the portals of our mind and heart, we connect to the realm of intuition and human spirit.

In dreams we are free. Free to love whomever we choose, to be reunited with loved ones, free to fly, to laugh, to visit other planets, other lives; in dreams we are the creators of our reality.

How awesome, vast and mysterious is the subject of dreams.

The information I will deal with in this infinite domain will be a mere chalk line on the blackboard of eternity, but I think you have the idea by now.

By tapping into dreams, we come into contact with the intelligence that is creating our lives. To understand that intelligence is to have a glimpse of the veiled holy face of life itself.

In sharing with you some of the dream material I have experienced, recorded and deciphered over the span of my life, you will be able to see how these dreams were a barometer of my innermost self, how my interpretation of these dreams helped me to a truer understanding of myself, and how I applied that understanding to the charting of my path in life.

The Avatars' Visit

When I was seventeen years old, I had this dream or spiritual experience.

I am standing in a white light so intense that I am aware only of the presence of the light. I look down and see that I am wearing a flowing white garment of some kind.

From within the brilliant white light, Jesus appears to greet me. He is smiling, holding a garland of flowers in his hand. He places the garland around my neck. I am ecstatic with happiness to see Him. He takes my hand and leads me through the white light. There is a Being with Him who radiates love and peace. I do not know who it is. Together they lead me to a circle of Beings, and we sit lotus-style among them in a perfect circle. Buddha is there, and others. I am overflowing with joy and perfect happiness in the presence of these Great Ones. There is such love, peace and goodness here. The white light is pervasive and intense. The feelings I am having go beyond any human means of expression. I listen as the Great Ones speak with me.

When I awaken, I have the feeling of having just experienced a separate reality, as if this were not a dream, but an actual happening or vision.

This dream was a mystical experience. The feeling and the memory of it are vivid and sustaining. It touched a chord within me of comfort, love and inner peace. In the light of my life's events, it continues to give me a feeling of faith, divine guidance and spiritual destiny.

Many times during the course of my life, when I became lost in the illusion of suffering, this "dream" would return as a memory to soothe and comfort me. In fact, so often dreams come into our conscious awareness as messages of support that help us reach a spiritual understanding within ourselves. They lend a sense of inner balance and patience that can see us through the rough spots in our lives.

On a Slide of Light

Early on my path, when I was groping in the dark for answers, I had this dream:

There is a slide projector out of which is projecting a brilliant beam of white light. A slide clicks into place illuminated by the white light. Why, it is a picture of me! The slide of myself clicks away, and only the white light is left, shining in a powerful radiant beam.

I "knew" immediately that the personality, "Angela," was a manifestation of the divine white light of the source of creation. The eternal white light was, in essence, who I am.

This dream was a confirmation of spiritual longings and feelings awakening within myself. At that time in my life, I would hang signs up in my house stating, "Slow down so you can speed up." I was feeling my way along without much support in my life or relationships. God came through in this dream and gave me support and information, the "knowing" I required to go forth. *Upon reflection, God has never let me down when I turned to Him in my need.*

I would like to share with you some dreams that have interceded and influenced my life's journey in a positive and effective way. Some of them were recurring dreams that warned me, in their ever-changing nature, of a pattern in my life that was destructive and needed to change. As I took the time to figure them out and connect them with my true feelings, they were able to have a truly transforming effect upon my consciousness, and thus upon the choices I made that influenced the course of my life. I find these dreams fascinating to explore, as they were really guides to me at crucial stages of my life when I was in emotional pain and my path was very difficult and not at all clear to me. Have you ever felt that way?

Then there were other dreams that were clearly giving me spiritual instruction and information. Another was a true psychic revelation, an answer to a prayer.

Many of the dreams recurred and changed over the course of time, as I changed. In fact, without the help of these dreams as reminders to me of my deepest, truest feelings, I probably would not have had the trust needed to go forward and make the necessary changes that healed my life.

These dreams charted the Way for me. You will be able to
see that the changes in each recurring dream reflected my inner
transformation—to have the courage and trust I needed as I
believed in the guidance I received and used it to change my
life. It worked!

I think that you will find these dreams interesting and
profound as I reveal them to you.

The Bakery

After my marriage, I began to have this dream:

> I am standing in front of a bakery, looking in the window.
> There are delicious eclairs, cakes and pies, cream puffs piled high
> with real whipped cream. I am aching with hunger looking
> through this window. I must have some of these luscious delica-
> cies! My mouth is salivating as I attempt to open the bakery door.
> I see my hand grasp the door knob and turn it back and forth. It
> is no use. The bakery door is locked.

As a child, I adored my father. However, he worked long
hours and was usually unavailable to me. Thus I sort of wor-
shipped him from afar and treasured the times we had together.
One such time was on Sundays, after church, when we would
go to the bakery together. It was such a treat for me! The
delectable smell of the rich desserts would fill my nostrils as we
entered the store. Then my father would allow me to pick out
anything I wanted—layer cake, lemon meringue pie, custard
donuts and fancy cookies; how I looked forward to this Sunday
treat. Without realizing it, I would fill my stomach with sweets
to make up for the attention I so needed and did not receive.
As a middle child, I spent much time alone, or taking care of
my brother and sister. The sweets in the bakery window were
symbolic of love to me.

When I married, I recreated some of my childhood feelings
by marrying a man who was there physically, but who was

emotionally unavailable to me. My childhood pain persisted as I inwardly craved the love and attention I did not receive. Again, I was relating to a dominant male figure from a distance, but this time there was abuse as well.

At the time of this dream, I was disconnected from my true self and unaware of my innermost feelings. I denied my pain and sought relentlessly to be "better" or "perfect," so that I could receive the love and caring I so desperately needed. This desperation registered as a physical hunger. The bakery symbolizes the love, attention and physical nurturing I needed from myself and from my relationship to fill the hunger. As you can see, in this dream I am locked out of the bakery. I am cut off from the love and food (nurturing) that would satisfy my inner need.

Upon reflection, the imagery that assisted in my healing of cancer, "the little birds eating golden crumbs," was symbolic of this need for love. Again, the cancer was symbolized by the buttery, golden crumbs.

I had this same dream for many years before I started to detach from my determination to get the love I needed from my husband, and began to look within myself to fill the need. It was very hard for me. I would make small strides and then cave in with guilt and remorse as the abuse heightened in the relationship, in a determined effort by my husband to stop the self-esteem and growth he sensed in me. However many times I would take a few steps and then fall on my face, I would get up and take a few steps more. My inner spirit was groping in the darkness, but somehow I persisted and change began to take place.

The Bakery #2

After many years, the dream changed. In fact, as I see it now, as I changed, so did the dream.

I am standing in front of the bakery, looking in the window at all the delicious cakes and pies. The eclairs and cream puffs,

piled high with fluffy whipped cream, are the most appealing. I
try the door of the bakery. It is locked. All of a sudden, a key
appears, an old-fashioned, ornate metal key. I turn it in the lock
and, lo and behold, the door opens! The ladies behind the
counter hail my entrance. What do I want? My wish is their
command. I eat old-fashioned crumb cake—it is scrumptious!
Then, one after another, I stuff myself with eclairs and cream
puffs. The ladies smilingly look on. They willingly encourage me
to eat, as I fill myself with the fluffy whipped cream.

I awake feeling as if I have gorged myself with pastries and
sweets. It is an actual feeling in my stomach; I am totally full.

At this time of my life, I was beginning to fully intuit the
meaning of the dream. There were problems within me regarding my self-esteem. There were definite problems in my marriage. I was becoming aware of my innermost feelings and needs
and taking action to help myself. I held the key to the bakery
door, which is the love and nurturing of myself. As I took action
in my life to give myself the love and support I needed, so my
intense inner hunger was filled and satisfied.

As I validated my feelings, I achieved a sense of self-worth
that gave me the confidence I needed to begin to make choices
on my own behalf. I began to assert myself in my life. After a
true moral struggle, I risked taking action to make me feel better
about myself. My self-respect increased. I was making progress.

The Bakery #3

I am standing in front of the bakery window. All the cakes
and pies are melting and running together like a Salvador Dali
painting. What is happening? I regard the melting cakes and
pies. The bakery window is dissolving. I become aware that I am
having a dream. I wake up.

Now that the dream had served its purpose, there was no
longer a need for it. My conscious mind had received the correct

message and appropriate action had been taken. The dream dissolved in conscious awareness.

I felt an increase of self-esteem as I honored my feeling self. I began to stand up for myself and take action in my relationships. My confidence increased as I realized that I was correctly assimilating unconscious messages and incorporating the wisdom I received in right action to improve my life.

That was the end of this dream, although it returns now and then in a very subdued version as a reminder to me if I am not honoring my needs. A few years ago, when I started a new relationship, it popped up again in this form:

The Bakery #4, in Miniature

I am asleep in my bed. Beneath the bed there is a mummy, buried under layers of dirt. When I get out of bed, I see that the dirt is beginning to crack on the surface. There is movement underneath! The mummy is rising! I leave the house to take a walk in the country, but the buried corpse follows me. Irritated, I finally turn around to take a look at it. It is definitely a mummy, trailing its tattered rags after it as it catches up with me. What does it want? I am not afraid of it, just irritated at its persistence. Finally I see that it is holding something out for me in its hand. I see that it is offering me a jelly donut. I laughingly refuse and go on my way.

As my old patterns of denying my feelings and needs in relationships began to emerge, my unconscious mind relayed an immediate message. I was not afraid to honor my needs, I just needed to be reminded. The jelly donut was just the right touch! I had this dream after a conversation with my mother about my true feelings, during which she shared some of her wisdom with me. That is why the buried corpse arose as a mummy. Thanks, Mommy!

The Cake, or Bakery #5

After ending the relationship with my first husband, who was so emotionally unavailable, and honoring my need for emotional depth and honesty in relationship, I had this dream:

> I am at a wedding. My father is cutting the wedding cake. He is smiling and joking with the wedding guests. I go to the front of the long line, thinking that my father will serve me before the other guests. I wait to get his attention, holding out my plate to be served. He sees me, but ignores me, serving the others. I stare at the cake. If he waits too long, there will be no more of the soft deep layers that are so delicious; only the top of the cake will be left, with all the hard, showy, fancy decorations. Finally, the last guest is served, and the inevitable happens: my father cuts me a piece off the top, covered in hard icing. He tells me it is the best piece because of all the decorations; there is a humorous glint in his eye. I become angry. I insist that IT IS NOT the best piece; it is hard, thin and inedible. In anger, I hurl it at the ground where it breaks into pieces. My father is surprised at this outburst, but I feel a right to my anger. I leave him and find, to my surprise, a beautiful large section of wedding cake with soft deep layers, carefully preserved, near a beautiful ocean. With joy I dip my fork into the depth of the layers, tasting and savoring the abundance. At long last, I feel worthy to receive the magnificent piece of cake I deserve—it is the best piece of all!

I was finally honoring my feelings in my relationships with men. I was honoring my right to depth, honesty, tenderness and love in relationship. My father was unable to convince me that superficiality is better than depth. He was unable to talk me out of my own feelings and perceptions. I *validated* my feelings and had the courage to express my anger. I then gave myself permission to let go of issues with my father that had been resolved. I was then able to honor my need for emotional nurturing and love in relationship. I had the courage to let go of my father and seek the unknown. A higher good awaited me as I now felt worthy to receive my good. I was free, at peace, fulfilled. I was ready for a higher order of relationship.

This dream *validated* the feelings I had acted upon in my life. I had ended a relationship that to me was lacking in depth, with a person who was only capable of limited emotional involvement. Without a doubt, I *knew* that many of the childhood issues that had been holding me back in life had been resolved. The wedding was a spiritual symbol of wholeness, bonding and communion. No longer was my father in command of the amount of love and nurturing that I required; now I had seized the reins of my life. I had risked the unknown. A gift awaited me, a gift of love and peace. This dream affirmed that the choice I had made at a critical juncture in my life was right.

The Tidal Wave

As a teenager, I began having this dream:

> I am at the beach. I am watching the water and I become alarmed. The waves are getting bigger and bigger. Suddenly all the water is sucked away and I see it in the distance—the tidal wave. It is awesome, momentous and alarming. I am in a panic but I cannot move! I try to run, but I am frozen to the spot! My heart beating wildly, I awaken.

I was becoming emotionally overwhelmed by my relationships and the circumstances of my life. I was mainly overwhelmed regarding male-female relationships. The emotions were awesome and overpowering. I was stymied in my ability to act. The situation was urgent and all-compelling. I was filled with fear, but I still did not have the ability to empower myself in the situation.

I realized eventually that my intense fear and lack of self-esteem was causing a failure to act on my own behalf. I was emotionally overwhelmed by my life. I began to read inspirational books and articles written by people who had changed their lives for the better. I gleaned hope from these stories of personal struggle and victory over all odds. I determined to conquer my fear, to acquire a sense of balance within myself and my relationships, and to succeed in my life. Gradually, I no longer felt paralyzed by fear and was able to incorporate positive action, which led to immense personal growth and change.

The Tidal Wave, #2

As I changed, the dream changed as well.

I am in Hawaii, driving on the highway near the ocean. Suddenly, I am aware that "the wave" is approaching. Way in the distance, I see it! If I take another route and drive fast enough, I will be able to avoid it. I press my foot on the accelerator.

I was aware that a positive direction was taking place in my personal growth, along with a redirection of my life. In taking action I was empowered in the presence of fear and powerful emotions. There was something I could do to help myself in the grip of overwhelming emotions and fear.

In letting go of fear, I was able to achieve a sense of emotional balance within myself and my relationships. Thus, I was able to make choices that affirmed my self-esteem.

The Tidal Wave, #3

I am in an enclosure underground. There are many workers here, and they are building an underground culvert. I speak with the foreman, and he shows me the strength of the construction. The foundation is immensely sturdy and resilient; we are very safe here. As we speak, I watch the men at work; they are relaxed, confident. I hear a hissing noise overhead and the foreman informs me that the wave has just hit. We are safe and dry beneath the strength of the culvert. There is nothing to fear.

Learning to love myself works! I was now strong, able to withstand emotional pressures with a sense of confidence and ease. My inner work had given me a strong foundation in the face of fear and emotional peril. I felt good about myself.

I was less fearful in my day-to-day life. I did not feel as overwhelmed as in the past by strong emotions and fears. The dream showed me I was growing. I was making progress.

The Tidal Wave, #4

I am in the ocean with a group of people. All of us are sporting helmets and elbow pads; we are holding onto surfboards for support. We are apparently here for sport. We are joking and laughing as we wait. I ask one of the players what we are doing here. He turns to me and tells me we are having tidal wave practice!

The unconscious certainly has a sense of humor! I was feeling a sense of expertise in my life. There was an acceptance and a command over overwhelming feelings and obstacles. I was beginning to enjoy a sense of play, a detachment from fear and more of a perception of life as a game that I could master and enjoy. The wry sense of humor in this dream helped me take charge of my life.

I never had the tidal wave dream again, thankfully! Years before, when I lived on the island of Guam, a tsunami alert was issued. We were all instructed to go to an area at the top of the island for safety. I was the first one there! Can you see how your greatest fears can become a reality? It is so worthwhile, then, to do the inner work required to address your fears and, in so doing, take charge of your life. There is nothing to fear, including fear itself!

The Baby

The honoring of my true feelings caused me to approach the point of separation from my husband. I was growing weary of the battleground that was my life with this man, and I was approaching a crossroads of real change. I took the children and left for New York to visit with my family and think things over. My husband called over and over again, asking me to come back, to give the marriage another try. Finally, I relented, against my better judgment, and returned. For a while, things were better. Then the old patterns began to take root again and I began to realize the hopelessness of the situation. It takes two to make a relationship work. One person can't do it all while the other fights for control. My despondency grew. One night I had this dream:

> I am in the cabin, when I become aware of a distant sound. I listen closely. There is a baby crying in the distance. I listen to the mournful cries and have a shock of realization. This is my baby! I have a baby, but have forgotten about it and now it is crying, probably starving! If I don't feed it and take care of it, it will die! In a panic, I search for the baby, but I cannot find it.

I had lost my true self in the illusion of suffering in my life. The change I had to make, the birth of my true self, had not been able to manifest. The birth had taken place, but now it had been forgotten and I was in pain again. The creative self was not being cared for or nurtured. If unattended, the opportunity for growth was going to die in the resistance to change.

This dream truly shocked me into the realization of the need for change. The feeling of the dream was urgent. I began once again to take stock of my situation and take back my own power.

The Baby #2

> I am in the cabin. Again, I hear the baby crying in the distance. Searching the cabin, I ascend the stairs. The crying is louder, though it is still muffled. I reach the bedroom, where I see a small coffin, shaped like a window seat, piled high with blankets. I approach the coffin and remove the blankets, with terror in my heart. Perhaps the baby is dead! But the cries grow louder as I remove the final blanket and open the lid. The baby smiles up at me, reaching up her arms for help. With great relief, I pull the baby out of the coffin and clasp it to my breast. I am so happy it is alive! I will do everything I can to take care of her and give her the love she needs to live!

The urgent message from my unconscious mind had been received and validated. Ascending the stairs represents the raising of my consciousness through the correct assessment of this information. The window seat represents my need to shed light on the situation. It was a window seat that I used to have in my room as a teenager, before I married my husband. The creative source had been buried, but now it was beginning to breathe once again. I knew I must change my life in order to love and nurture myself.

Through the feelings I experienced as a result of this dream, I made a decision to leave my marriage. Unknowingly, I had already manifested the disease of cancer. I took the painful, arduous necessary steps to extricate myself from the marriage and take care of the baby, my Authentic Self.

The Baby #3

> I am sitting, holding the baby, when she leaps from my arms and begins to crawl on the floor. At first I am afraid for her, because she is not old enough to crawl, but then something unexpected occurs. The baby jumps to her feet and begins to run

around, laughing and performing acrobatic feats for me! I never knew the baby was capable of this! This baby is a genius!

My Authentic Self was capable of so much more than I ever imagined possible! I was gaining a sense of trust in myself and true self-esteem. My belief in my abilities was growing with each step I took to incorporate my values into my life. I felt good about who I am!

This amazing dream gave me support and encouragement when I needed it most. I began to truly see that "As I Love and Support Myself, So Does God and the Universe Support Me."

The Baby #4

After the doctor told me I had cancer, I had this dream while undergoing radiation treatments in the hospital:

> I am holding the baby, walking through the white light. I am in a mansion of sorts. There is a beautiful room with ornate stone pillars before me. All is bathed and softened in a peaceful, healing white light. I see my sister-in-law Caryl (deceased from cancer a few years prior) bathing in the healing waters of the pool. She is smiling radiantly, dressed in a flowing white robe. She beckons to me. I approach her and she holds out her arms to take the baby. She bathes the baby playfully and lovingly in the healing waters, her face wreathed in smiles of joy. She tells me that she is helping me take care of the baby. I am so happy to see her! I have missed her so much! She smiles again. There is so much love emanating from her that this room is filled with the presence of light and love and healing. She tells me again not to worry; she will help me take care of the baby.

I believe this dream was a mystical experience. I am convinced that the people we love and who have loved us help us "from the other side" and give us guidance and support. The beauty and supportive pillars of the mansion represent a purity and strength of consciousness. The healing waters represent love, support and healing messages from the unconscious mind.

The feeling of this dream was one of overwhelming love, comfort and peace. I had a true sense of being divinely protected and guided on my path in life. The memory of this "dream" was of unearthly comfort and support, and it sustained me with faith in myself and God. It gave me a belief that I could heal the illness, and that I was receiving divine help and guidance in doing so.

As you know, I did heal from cancer that first time, and the next time as well. Every day, my love of myself grew, my faith in God was a rock and a sustenance, and compassion for my fellow man was born and actualized.

The Baby #5

Just a few months ago, I had this dream:

I am walking down the street with my baby in my arms. It is one of the older streets in New York, similar to where I lived as a little girl. I am absolutely thrilled about this baby as I cuddle it close to me, enjoying my walk. When I look into the baby's eyes, it winks back at me in total empathy. The baby is cooing and singing, and I am singing with her, joyfully imitating her sounds. The baby is so happy, so sweet and darling; I am in love with this baby! People pass us as we walk, smiling and gesturing to one another. This is not the important thing. What is important is how much I love this baby, and how happy I am! The feeling of love is utter ecstasy as my baby and I bounce up the stairs and enter the living room of our abode. The living room is filled with exotic treasures and fascinating artifacts from all over the world. There are precious items of jewelry and carved statues from Egypt and Africa. Gorgeous oil paintings hang on the walls. As I gaze upon the beauty and wonder of all these treasures, my sense of hope and optimism, my curiosity about life and living things is limitless and boundless! I am so happy to be alive!

This dream is practically self-explanatory and reveals the love and inner peace I have found within my own being. My Authentic Self is being loved and valued. There is oneness, empathy, wholeness and unity. The dream has a total feeling of unconditional love. The "living room" represents my conscious-ness, and the universal fascination, joy and fulfillment I feel in my work and in my life. Life is awesome, filled with the spirit of adventure.

This dream helped me to realize my state of mind and what I had achieved within myself in terms of inner peace and self-esteem. It helped me gain a healthy perspective of myself, a feeling of accomplishment regarding my life and work, and an authentic connection with God as unconditional love and peace.

As I look back, I can see that the path of my life was somehow mapped out in my dreams. Had I chosen to ignore these unconscious messages, I cannot imagine where I would be today, or even if I would still be alive. Paying attention to my dreams has helped me so much. The guidance I have received has truly been of invaluable significance to my life and well-being.

A Message from the Book of Life

I would be remiss if I did not include in this chapter one of the most powerful dreams I have ever experienced. It happened at the end of a very complex and meaningful relationship that ended on a note of ambiguity, which I found hard to accept without further explanation. Try as I might, I could not deter-mine why the relationship had not worked out. I just could not figure it out, accept it and go on with my life. Such was my mental and emotional anguish that I turned to God for help. I had read the words of a spiritual master who stated that if we turn to God with an innermost cry from the heart, that God would not fail to answer. One night, before going to sleep, I turned to God in such a manner. I begged Him to give me some information that would bring comfort to me and allow me to let go of the situation. I said this prayer as a true cry from the heart before falling asleep. That night, I had this dream.

> I saw before me a pair of spiritual hands, which I thought to be the hands of God. I could actually hear a heavenly choir of angelic voices, a phenomenon I have never witnessed before or since. As the angelic voices grew stronger, I saw that the hands were holding a book. I was instructed to observe the title. This was the book of my life! The book opened; pages were turned. The instructing finger pointed to a chapter; it directed me to read one of the inscribed lines. The book stated: "The reason your relationship did not work out is that it was not in the curlings."

I immediately woke up. It was still nighttime. My heart was beating fast; I was excited. I knew this was the answer to my prayer. But what did it mean? What did the word *curlings*, mean? I went downstairs and made myself a cup of coffee. I sat at the kitchen table, looking out the window, waiting for daylight, reflecting upon the message I had received.

At nine o'clock sharp I telephoned my girlfriend, who was the town librarian. I asked her if she had ever heard of the word, "curlings." She paused a moment and said it sounded familiar, but she would research it and call me back.

About an hour later she called to tell me she had located the word. It was an ancient word meaning fate, or destiny. Many centuries ago, people used to go places to have their fortunes told. The person reading the fortune would snip off a lock of hair. When the "curlings" fell to the ground, the fortune teller would read them, similar to tea leaves.

There was no way on earth I could have ever known the meaning of that word. This was information, somehow stored in the universal mind, that had emerged as information in my dream. It had an immediate and calming effect on me. This was an answer I could accept. If it was in fact an act of fate or destiny that this relationship was not meant to be, then I must let go of it and move on. Once again, the deep inner chord, the chord of truth, had been struck. I felt a deep sense of peace, a calm acceptance, an infinite sense of gratitude toward the all-knowing intelligence that had taken mercy on me and gifted me with an answer. I thanked God for his infinite goodness, kindness, love and mercy.

After this "answer," I was able to let go of the past and go forward in my life. In forgiving myself for not being perfect, I was able to accept the fact that I could not control all facets of my existence. I felt very strongly the presence of a divine order governing humankind and all living things. This presence had nothing to do with the intellect or the rational mind. I realized a great truth: that in all our actions, all our relationships, we can do just so much, and the rest we must let go to God. This does not mean an abdication of responsibility, but taking up a total personal responsibility and a responsibility toward life itself, to intuit the meaning of experiences, and to have the humility to accept human limitations, while aspiring to be that which is aware, beautiful, good, loving and valuable.

The Dreamer in the Cabin

Have you ever come awake in a dream and realized you were dreaming? This experience is known as *lucid dreaming*. It is the maintaining of conscious awareness in the midst of a dream. In the exploration of the self, there are no boundaries.

I would like to share an experience with you that illustrates this point. Many years ago, when I lived in a log cabin in Canada, I decided to experiment with dreaming. I had read a book by Carlos Castaneda, wherein Don Juan, a Yaqui Indian "man of knowledge," had given Carlos a technique to stimulate conscious awareness in dreaming. The technique he advised was to focus attention on one's hands when coming awake within the dream. In this manner, he suggested, a person could actually maintain awareness within the dream state without waking up into normal everyday reality. I decided to try this technique myself.

It was not as easy as one might think. After giving the powerful suggestion to my mind to awaken within the dream by focusing on my hands, I had dream after dream of searching for a pair of gloves. I would then find the gloves, put them on, and stare fixedly at my hands. I would then wake up. This went on for many weeks.

One morning, I awoke, only to fall asleep again. I then began to dream. I dreamed I was downstairs in the kitchen of the cabin, arranging flowers in a vase on the windowsill. I looked out the window and noticed it was a stormy autumn day. I then regarded the flowers in the vase and realized dimly that they were summer wild flowers. Something clicked within me and it was as if time suspended for an instant. I became aware that I was dreaming. I then began to wake up, but remembered to focus my attention on my hands. As I did so, I again became "awake" within the dream. I had the shocking realization: "I'm awake! This is a dream, but I'm awake!" It was exciting! I then found myself literally bouncing back and forth from wall to wall as if I were swimming. I had another awareness: "This is what I used to do as a child!"

Then my awareness began to recede. I quickly "willed" myself over to the fireplace and instantly found myself standing there, trying to look up at the loft, where I knew my body was sleeping. It was hard to look up; fear kept forcing my head the other way, but I finally did look up and see myself "asleep" on the bed. My body seemed to be made of light. I then had a moment of panic in the thought that perhaps I would not be able to get back to my body.

Instantly I found myself horizontal, "floating" upwards toward the ceiling, to where my body lay in the bed above me. I was in continuous awareness as I floated up. As I reached the ceiling, the thought went through me, "Can I actually go through the ceiling?" And yes, upwards through the ceiling I floated.

The next moment found me aware of being back in my body. The thought came to me that as I entered my body, it felt as if my body were "infused with light." I opened my eyes. I did not feel as if I had been dreaming. I felt as if the intelligence within me was aware of having had an actual experience. I felt very calm and peaceful. I felt as if I was learning something deeply valuable about myself.

That evening, while chopping vegetables in the kitchen for a stew, I looked at my hands chopping the vegetables and had a shock of awareness throughout my body. This time I felt as if the dreamer were dreaming me. In other words, I felt as if I myself were a dream in the mind of the Creator. This was an astounding awareness. I left the kitchen and went for a walk outdoors. I put my feet in the waters of the flowing brook outside my door and allowed myself to be filled with the wonder and beauty that surrounded me. I again had the "knowing" that all of life is an awesome mystery. I was humbled to be a part of the mystery and to be able to experience one particle of this incredible adventure that is my journey on this earth.

The Man in Black

Recently I have begun dreaming of a man in black. I could make no connection at all to this dream, but it drew a powerful response within me.

After I finished writing this book, I began having this dream. It turned out to have a powerful significance, so I am including it here.

> There is a man in black waiting for me in the shadows. He sends me a letter, but my cat has torn it up and I cannot read it. I try putting the pieces together in desperation to read what is written, but it is of no avail. The letter has fallen apart at the fold lines, like the piece of paper I found in the old wallet

mentioned at the start of this book, upon which was written, "Because of my faith in this miracle I am escaping."

The man in black silently waits in the shadows.

As I strove inwardly to intuit the meaning here, the increased responsibilities of my life propelled me forward to make choices and decisions in areas of life I had never explored before and which, in fact, I had always disliked and resisted. Decisions in business, publishing, expansion of my personal and work life and, all important, the focus to fulfill myself and grow. There was a radical shift away from finding happiness in relationship with a man to expanding myself as a human being to find the love and peace I needed in my life. Could the piece of folded paper mean I am realizing the "miracle" for which I "escaped" nine years before?

The Man in Black #2

I speak to the Man in Black over the phone. The joy and ecstasy I feel are unparalleled—I have finally found "The One."

I still cannot connect or relate in any way to the dream. I want to believe it is a man I will meet, but I know it is not. My mother tells me she believes that somehow *I* am the man in black.

I go forward in my life and work and make courageous changes that are necessary to ensure my values in life. My children have become a priority. I do not have enough time to spend with them. I begin cutting down the hours of my practice and moving more into workshops so I can be with them more. This is a risk, but my priorities are changing and so must I. Somehow events shape themselves to support these changes. I am going on faith, asking for help in all areas. My office building is demolished and I find a new space in a professional building where the other tenants are all medical doctors. I am invited into the building with honor and respect by the medical profession. My office is now on the third floor of a professional building—an affirmation of positive growth.

Man in Black #3

I am in a trailer in the woods with the man in black. I am so in love with him. I never intended to fall in love with a man in black, but I accept it. The ecstasy I feel when with him is worth the ostracism I might receive.

I am loving and accepting myself unconditionally even though I am needing to open up and reach out for the help I need. I am asking God for help as well as letting go to God.

I am in spiritual transformation once again, making a tremondous leap of faith. It is again literally a death and rebirth. I am stretching the limits of myself to encompass the energy needed to make dramatic changes. The risk pulls resources from myself heretofore untapped. Pain flows forth from childhood feelings of rejection. I go forth, it seems, on faith alone.

Once again, I am "stopping the world" to create a new reality. Startling changes are occurring. I am opening to receive psychic phenomena that I have not been able to witness before. I feel alone.

The Man in Black #4

I am sitting in a waiting room with a cat. I grow tired of waiting. Picking up the cat in my arms, I leave the waiting room.

"I don't have a degree," I say aloud.

"I do," says a calm, authoritative voice. I turn to see the man in black who has spoken. He is out of the shadows, illuminated in the light. He is still dressed in black, but I can see him clearly. He is serene, yet a mystery.

I awaken. I know this is an important dream. It is saying the man in black is the authority and can help me. I long to know the meaning of this figure with all my heart.

That night I go out on the pier behind my house. I look out at the starry sky and ask God to solve my problems. I can no longer do it alone. I need God's help. I ask God to take it all, just as I did years ago before the healing.

Feeling calmer, I go inside the house. I actually have a moment to do nothing. It feels good, but the feeling of respon- sibility is painful. Aimlessly I open a cabinet I have not looked in for quite some time. I see a section of a paperback lying on the shelf. Without thinking, I pick it up. The title startles me: *Heroes and Hero-Makers*.

A chill runs up my spine. I sit down to read.

The writer is depicting the life of the heroic path. He states that, at a certain level of growth, the individual grows from an individualized consciousness into one of community service. At this time, the trials on the path are truly arduous and archetypes are needed. The unconscious mind sends forth symbols to assist the hero. An example of a dream is given. I catch my breath as I read on: "A young man in black stands up and I think he must be the true hero," and, "The dreamer could offer no association to the man in black."

The author goes on to say that the man in black represents the true, authentic self, the spiritual self. Tears fill my eyes as I give gratitude to God. I search to find the missing book from which this piece belongs. I find it: *Man and His Symbols* by Carl Jung.

Once again, I am young and believe in miracles. Seemingly my whole life, my whole path, this whole book is being affirmed for me. I smile through the tears in gratitude and awe for the miracle that is my life. Once again the Beloved is winking his eye at me, affirming my faith, saying, "Do not Fear. I am with you."

Thank you Lord. Amen.

There! I've titillated your imagination, haven't I? If so, I am glad, so glad to spur you on to believe in yourself enough to explore the awesome mystery of who you are.

I could go on relating experiences in dreaming that I have had and the wisdom many of my clients have gleaned from writing down their dreams and taking the time and interest to interpret them.

As you can see, my dreams have been valuable tools for me in gaining an insight into my true inner feelings. This insight has helped me to make choices on the part of myself that led to astounding changes in my life. Changes for the better! To be sure, these choices took risk, but what in life is gained without risk of some kind? Without risk, life becomes dull and boring. Have the courage to take part in your life and live!

I have found *Edgar Cayce's Dreams,* by Mark Thurston, to be a really valuable guide to the interpretation of dreams. Robert Monroe, author of *Journeys Out of the Body,* and founder of the Monroe Institute in Virginia, has given us fascinating insights into the awareness of "out of body" experience. Monroe's courageous accounts offer valuable information to the student of life who is willing to open the doors of perception and expand into new conceptions of time/space reality.

Investigate your dreams and help solve the puzzle that is your life on this earth. Why live eternally in an inner conflict that drains your energy, when you can take steps to learn more about yourself and be empowered to make the right choices, the elegant healing choices, that will lead you to your ultimate highest good? Why go on in fear and ignorance when there are vast frontiers of mystery within your own self, just waiting to be tapped into and explored?

I hope that you have enjoyed this chapter. I certainly have enjoyed writing it! I am confident that you will allow these words to encourage you to step forth out of fear and into the belief that life can truly be wonderful—and that you deserve a happy, loving, peaceful, prosperous life.

Use the following exercise and affirmations, or the *Hammock of Light* meditation at the end of the book, to help open up the rich world of dreams for yourself.

Exercise:

Start a dream log. Keep your log by the bed and record your dreams as soon as you wake up, so that you will remember them. Seeing your dreams written down in black and white will give them validity. See whether you can figure out the symbols and messages of your dreams, and how they apply to your life. Not only is this fun, but it is exciting to uncover the hidden information that will help you chart your path in life. Good Luck!

Affirrmations:

๛ It is safe for me to remember my dreams.

๛ It is safe for me to explore within myself.

๛ I open myself to receive the wisdom of the Universe for use as guidance and direction in my life.

10

By their fruits, you shall know them.

—Jesus

Motivation and the DNA Helix

In all human action lies a seed of truth called motivation.

Motivation is the DNA within the seed of an idea that determines the outcome of an action. As a ripe, healthy seed grows into lush, flourishing plant life or graceful, flowering, magnificent trees, so does damaged, defective seed produce life that is deformed, ineffective, destructive and unhealthy.

In all action, we must be aware of our motivation. Only then can we know the truth of our actions, be assured that our healthy seed yields luscious, bountiful fruit, and take charge of our lives.

Most of us are hard at work concocting the purest of motivations for actions based on greed, jealousy or hatred.

We are intent on controlling everything and everyone in our lives. In this manner, we hurt and injure our husbands, wives, children, friends and family. We loudly proclaim our innocence while defusing the energy and power of those closest to our hearts. Instead of fostering freedom and independence in ourselves and others, we seek to hold them fast through manipulation and control.

We are then shocked to find our lives filled with crucial problems such as alcohol and drug addiction, sexual promiscuity and serious illness.

We ourselves become deeply hurt and dissatisfied with ourselves and our relationships. We lead existences of ignorance and suffering instead of balanced, healthy lives.

Only through the honesty of inner struggle can we assess the truth of our motivations and improve the quality of our lives.

Only through the purest goodness inherent in our motivation can we truly love ourselves and have compassion for our fellow human beings or feel happy for the success of another's life, instead of envious, competitive and in constant comparison, critical and dissatisfied with our own selves.

There is a simple truth here: our lives simply **do not work** unless the motivation for our actions is unsullied by negativity and ugliness, greed, jealousy and envy, anger, guilt or fear.

The DNA, the motivation in the seed for action that creates a joyful, healthy life, can only be one thing: LOVE.

Love is the only pure motivation.

That love must be for one's own self and one's fellow human beings. This is the *only way out* of life's suffering.

I have learned this through harsh experience. In fact, all that I am teaching here has been learned through my own life experience. I did not read it in a book and then espouse it. As a student of life, I *live* this way. That is how I know it works.

Only by taking the risk to live your truth can you live a magnificent, heroic life, feeling the pure essence of love and truth flowing limitlessly within yourself and having a boundless supply to offer to others.

It has been a long and rocky road for me; life and God had to hit me painfully with the Zen stick before I finally woke up and took the time, caring, attention and love to honestly assess my thoughts, words and deeds, and become an obedient child of God: *there is no other way to live and be happy.*

I apologize to you that life is this way—it is irritating, is it not—that we must be responsible for our thoughts, beliefs, words and actions? That it is all up to us?

But the crucial point here is that, unless we assume the responsibility for our lives, *we will keep on suffering!*

There is no other way out. All attempts to escape this responsibility through entertainment, television, alcohol, drugs or sex only leads us back to the pain in ourselves.

Take a moment to reflect on the enormity of this information. Are you yawning, wanting to escape by falling asleep in resistance to this truth? Or do you feel an acceptance, a hunger in yourself to know more? Once responsibility has been accepted, life becomes a whole lot easier.

Now, let us continue.

Have you ever wondered why things didn't work out as you planned? Part of the reason, I believe, is the divine right order of the Universe—fate or destiny; the other part is you—you and your motivation. A story illustrates this point:

There once was a man who lived his life and died a peaceful death. When he reached the Pearly Gates, he heard a voice asking, "What have you done with your life?" The man could not answer the question. He did not know what it meant. The voice told him that he could not enter the Pearly Gates and must return to earth as a baby and live life once again, living life the right way. The man did not understand, but was reborn, and this time lived life peacefully and filled with good deeds that drew praise from other men.

He again died peacefully. Again, as he demanded entrance through the Pearly Gates, a voice asked him, "What have you done with your life?" This time he understood, he thought, and began to reiterate his good deeds and services. The Pearly Gates remained closed to him. In frustration, the man wailed to the Lord, "Why?"

The Lord said calmly, "Go back and try again. You did the right thing for the wrong reason." If we continually deceive ourselves about our motivation, we remain within the illusion of suffering that has become a way of life on this planet.

To emerge from that suffering, we must come into the light of truth. Inherent in the light of this truth is the realization and acceptance of our humanness. We are human. Therefore, we are capable of both good and evil. If we deny our capacity for evil and misconduct, then we are denying the human part of ourselves and living a lie.

As human beings, we are fully capable of anything and everything. In realizing that painful feelings such as jealousy, envy, greed, hatred, dishonesty, anger, fear and guilt are part of who we are, we are then able to own them, view them without judgment and move out of them.

This movement, this viewing of the imperfect in ourselves without judgment, is love. It is what loving ourselves is all about. Only in coming out of the judgment of our own imperfect selves can we move into a higher order of being—one of loving and perfecting ourselves, our relationships and our lives.

The movement of awareness of our humanness, without judgment, is love. Can you see the tremendous power we have at every moment to choose either love and trust, or fear and doubt? Can you see how that choice creates our very lives and destinies?

The Last Judgment

Years ago, my brother visited me, accompanied by his new girlfriend. In the course of the conversation, it was revealed that this woman did not have the custody of her children. The thought went through my mind, "What kind of a mother could she be, having lost the custody of her children?"

My friends, I can honestly tell you that this was the last judgment I ever made. SLAM! Down came the Zen stick for the final blow, when, as a devoted mother, I lost the custody of my own children! God finally got the point across to me! It was then that I truly felt the words of Jesus as a living truth for me, "Judge not, lest ye be judged."

It was at this point that the critic within me went down for the final time, crying, "Uncle! I'm dead!"—and I'm so glad that critic is dead, because at that time, I was born. It took a lot of inner work and a bout with cancer afterwards, plus tremendous moral inventory and forgiveness, but I finally reached a point where I truly felt a deep acceptance and love for myself and others. I became capable of true unconditional love and compassion.

Service to others helped a lot. In fact, that was when, after volunteering in the cancer ward of the hospital, I founded Self-Healing.

When I founded Self-Healing, I realized the absolute necessity for complete honesty in all undertakings. So I asked myself this question: what is the motivation for my project?

I turned inward and became clear within myself.

My motivations were:

1. To give the love I could no longer share on an everyday basis with my children to my fellow human beings. I had so much love—it had to go somewhere, every day, so I decided to share it with others.

2. To help both myself and others through giving that love. Sharing felt awesomely good! I realized that the giving and sharing of truth and love is what I was born for. It is as natural to me as a flower that blooms or a bird that soars freely in the sky.

3. To grow and learn, to impart, through love and wisdom, health and healing to myself and others.

4. To manifest, in right livelihood, the wisdom and prosperity I need to live the fullest and most wonderful life imaginable; to share this love, wisdom and prosperity with my children, to offer healing sustenance to them for my responsibility in their suffering, and to help heal their lives.

To dedicate myself to assisting in the healing of this beautiful planet upon which we live, along with the human beings who are responsible for and who inhabit this planet.

Did you notice how the love of myself was at the root of the motivation and, after that, the love of mankind? And you see, that is the reason why, with the help of God, this all worked out so miraculously for me, and why it can for you as well.

You can see how one human being can empower him or herself, and thus benefit not only themselves and their families, but all of mankind.

The Power of One

Once, many years ago, I was watching two carpenters in a tiny rowboat paint the hull of a huge sailing ship. In fact, the ship was the *Bounty*, from the movie, *Mutiny on the Bounty*, which is on exhibit in St. Petersburg, Florida. One of the carpenters stood up in the rowboat and, with the index finger of his hand, showed that he could actually move the ship in the water! He kept laughing and pushing the ship with his index finger, and the ship would actually move!

Many of the patrons were laughing, watching this fellow, and I was watching him too, but I was not laughing. Instead, I was experiencing a powerful realization. One man, I thought, with all the circumstances aligned in the proper order, could tremendously influence events in his favor. In other circumstances, this carpenter could not move that ship an iota with his index finger, yet, somehow, here and now, with all things in a certain arrangement and his awareness of that arrangement being right, he was empowered.

The carpenter, without realizing it, taught me a valuable lesson that day.

You are important. How you think, what you believe and how you conduct yourself affects not only you, but those nearest and dearest to you; in fact, the lives of everyone here on earth are touched by you—including this wounded planet upon which we live.

Make that touch be one of love, peace and healing.

This is the power you have. Take responsibility for it, and use it to help and heal. Why else are we born, if not for this reason? To learn how to love is our greatest lesson here on earth. Can you imagine what kind of world it would be if each human being took on the responsibility of his or her life and came forth out of fear into love?

After I founded Self-Healing, the seed of my loving motivation began to bear beautiful fruit. A marvelous miracle began to occur. As I expressed the love on a daily basis that I could no longer give to my children, I began to see the faces of my children in my clients! Some nuance or gesture, manner or look, would remind me of one or the other of my three beloved boys.

How happy this made me! It felt as if my children were near to me at every moment. I knew then that the love I was giving was coming back to me and that this is a true spiritual law.

What you give, returns to you. What goes around, comes around.

Make what you give be the purest of love. Give freely, without expectation of reward. Only then does that love return to you in its purest and deepest form and create a heaven within yourself and in all that you touch and do. That heaven you are creating is your life!

The Sacred Affirmation of the DNA Helix

One day, a few years ago, I was at the beach with my friend, Carol Jean. We were enjoying the glorious day, the sparkling water, when I noticed something unusual in the sky.

I pointed it out to Carol Jean, and we both looked up to get a better view. Up, way up in the distant reaches of the sky, was a slowly spinning spiral of birds. The birds appeared small from our point of view, but they were indeed a flock of pelicans. However, they had arranged themselves in a most unusual formation. Slowly rotating in the air currents, the spiral of pelicans formed a shape I knew from science to be none other than the DNA Helix. "Carol Jean!" I cried, searching my memory. "That spiral they are forming—it is most definitely a helix! The DNA helix!"

We laughed in excitement and stared at one another in awe. Neither one of us had ever seen a formation of birds arranged so perfectly, so precisely in a helix form. The definitive spiralling roll of the helix of birds removed all doubt from the mind that this was indeed a helix; it made an astounding spectacle in the sky. We marveled about it, pondering its meaning. It was a most amazing sight.

In the next few weeks, upon looking out the window of my office, we again spotted the spiralling helix of birds. Again, we marveled and wondered at the meaning of this unusual occurrence.

A few months later, I read a book by Ken Carey, *Return of the Bird Tribes*. In this book, Carey asserts that humankind is going through an evolutionary shift of the healing of consciousness. According to Indian legend, ancient spirits of angels and beings of light and wisdom long removed from planetary influence are now returning to earth to elevate human consciousness and assist in the healing of the planet and all of mankind.

Carey states that these ancient spirits were once in earthly form, but they transcended into the ether due to the predominance of violence and ignorance resulting from the rise of the ego in man, which resulted in the fall from grace of the human spirit.

These beings, or Bird Tribes of Indian legend, are now returning to earth in large numbers to initiate a radical transformation in human consciousness, and thus ensure the survival of the planet and species.

Carey further states that the source of this transformation is taking place right now, in the genetic structure or DNA of each of those human beings whose destiny it is to help alleviate the suffering of humanity and to assist in the healing of the planet.

The genetic triggers now being awakened within the DNA of each of these human beings is causing a complete revolution and transformation of each human life in the direction of a higher good for all of mankind.

In the Indian legend, the sacred spiral is a symbol for DNA.

A few weeks later, one of my clients brought me a manual he had found in Colorado that affirmed this basic assertion. Somewhere within me, the chord of truth was struck again, that deep resonance within me that is somehow humorous, simple, complex, informative and mystical all at the same time. Truly, "the Beloved" was once again winking his eye, saying, "I love you. I am always present for you, eternally offering protection and guidance to you on your path."

At this moment, I smile as I write these words, realizing that all signs and information are given to us at each and every moment in life. It is all there in the world around us, if we but look, see and believe.

These signs light our path in life with faith if we choose to believe in them. The messengers are for the child-like and the innocent, the innovators, the shakers and movers, the believers that life is truly a course in miracles.

I choose to be one of these people.

Before doing the "Art of Living" workshop with Bernie Siegel, an article about Bernie and myself appeared in the newspaper. Directly beneath the article, as large as life was a large drawing of the DNA Helix.

Coincidence? Coincidence, Bernie says, is God's way of remaining anonymous. I leave it to you to ponder and decide, and to reflect on your motivations.

11

Amazing grace, how sweet the sound, that saved a
wretch like me. I once was lost, but now am found,
was blind but now I see.

—John Newton

Addiction

The source of all addiction is the state of being internally cut off from God's love.

We turn to a substitute to fill the need for that love—alcohol, drugs, sex, food, money, work—and find that we are only escaping through that substance the pain and suffering of an unfulfilled need for love and emotional bonding. We seek to receive fulfillment of this deep hunger for love and bonding through the outside source.

We cannot acquire through any external source or substitute, however stimulating for the moment, the nurturing and sustenance we receive in the experience of love.

As children, we sought love, nurturing and emotional bonding with adults incapable of fulfilling the requirement of true unconditional love.

As addicts, we continually seek to fill that need through an outside source. Whether it be alcohol, drugs, food, sex, money, work or another human being, we never receive what we need. Therefore, we habitually return to that substance or person time and time again, trying relentlessly and fruitlessly to fulfill ourselves.

Through living in this compulsive and driven manner, we become helpless addicts who literally believe our lives depend on an outside source for survival.

We become confused, dependent, and miserable human beings, resentful of one another; we seek to gratify and fill ourselves up with outside stimulation in order to survive.

In literally living out the belief that we are dependent on this outside source for our very survival, we live in denial of the true reality of who we are and what life is all about. We lose ourselves in the lie that has become all that we know of life—abject suffering—the antithesis of true joy, peace, and love.

Any human being who is cut off from the light and love of God lives in darkness. In this darkness is ignorance and suffering. In this darkness lies evil, which is nothing more than the absence of light.

Being cut off from God's love is the source of all human misery.

Being cut off from God's love is not a tragic accident that befalls the addict. It is an ACT OF WILL. It is the act of turning from the light and love of God toward the Iron Will of Ignorance, or ego.

This Iron Will of Ignorance, as I mentioned earlier, is none other than the intellectual mind run rampant in the human being. In this state, a human being is cut off from feeling and love, and is driven at all times to be *in control*.

In fact, a human being in the state of addiction is in total *fear of love*.

You can see how an addict makes choice after choice based on the Iron Will of Ignorance, and the need to be in control at all times. In this manner, addicts destroy their own lives, and are destructive to all those who surround them.

In exercising the need to be in control, addicts become exceedingly manipulative and cunning in order to have Their Way.

Addicts use *control* to avoid feelings of powerlessness. As a means of control addicts employ various methods:

- sex
- money
- intimidation
- anger
- guilt
- shame
- criticism
- withdrawal
- rejection

Do these feel familiar? Perhaps you have felt the effects of these methods of control in an area of your body—the stomach, for instance. Have you ever felt suddenly sick to your stomach? Felt like you were being kicked or hit in the stomach? Had sudden bouts of sickness and vomiting without knowing why?

Perhaps you are feeling the effects of one or more of these control mechanisms. I have worked with women who have manifested such physical symptoms in addictive relationships. I have experienced these feelings myself. They are not pleasant. These physical reactions are felt as a result of having your human will sublimated by the Iron Will of Ignorance. Does this sound scary? It is—frightening and exceedingly painful. Over the course of time, this emotional abuse can court illness in the body.

Men and women who indulge in sexuality without the attendant feelings of affection, love, tenderness, caring and commitment are abusing their emotions and their bodies. The pattern of sexuality without feeling is rampant in today's society and a major addiction. Interestingly enough, since so many of us are out of touch with our feelings, we are unconscious of these addictive patterns of sexuality; therefore, addiction passes for love. But it is not love; it is addiction.

Once these destructive patterns are unearthed through awareness, we can feel the misery and suffering we are hiding behind and, through love of ourselves, heal our addictions. We must, through our unbending intention, invite love and feeling into our lives. We must not settle for less.

I am using the word addict; however, most of us in the present society are addicts of one sort or another. Since the latest statistics show that over ninety-eight percent of our population is dysfunctional, you can see how the problem of addiction is a major affliction of the society in which we live.

Since the source of addiction is the state of being cut off from God's love, a person in this mode lives in darkness, removed from truth and light. The individual is therefore in a state of delusion, or denial, fighting tooth and nail to maintain a way of life that has become a LIE.

Since vulnerability and love are terrifying to the addictive personality, there is a need to maintain obsessive thought patterns, a need to be in thought, like a hamster on a wheel, at all times. Worry and fear can also become addictions.

The only freedom from obsessive thought is found in the substance, whether it be sex, drugs, alcohol, food, money or material objects. The "substance," can even be another human being, as illustrated in the problem of co-dependency, where a person is "used" by the addict to escape responsibility.

The need to escape the responsibility of his or her own life is the key focus of the addictive personality. The addict, therefore, in many cases uses another human being as a "food source" to fuel and supply an overwhelming need to be in control, so that he or she will not experience *abandonment*.

Taken to the extreme, we have the case of Jeffrey Dahmer, the Milwaukee serial killer who actually used his victims' bodies as a food source. A video tape of a psychiatrist who interviewed Dahmer revealed that, as a teenager after his parent's divorce, Dahmer became terrified of abandonment. His first murder was committed trying to prevent a male companion from "leaving him."

The psychiatrist found him surprisingly open, honest and agreeable. This is the deceptive "flip-side" of the addict. They are experts at manipulation.

Dahmer was a sex addict who believed that consuming the bodies of his victims would internalize their souls within his body. In this way, he would never be alone. His victims could not leave him. He surrounded himself with the skulls and bones of those he slayed. These bones gave him a sense of comfort and protection. He was in control. This is addiction taken to its ultimate insane extreme.

David Koresh is another example of the Iron Will of Ignorance taken to its full-blown maximum.

Koresh, a sex addict and leader of the cult Branch Davidian in Texas, was able to convince a legion of followers that he was a man of God, indeed, that he *was* God. This is the wily expertise of the addict at having the right words at the right time to convey a most convincing pretense of innocence. Only the appropriate feelings and actions are missing. Somehow the feelings and actions are wrong.

Koresh named his compound, where he and his disciples lived, "Apocalypse." Sadly, this turned out to be a tragic omen of his destructive path which turned into a flaming apocalypse at the end. He would rather destroy himself and everyone else than *submit his will*.

This is addiction taken to the end of the line, to extremes of darkness.

Dahmer and Koresh are examples of how slick, wily, cunning and convincing addicts can be. They are masters at maintaining their will, the **Iron Will of Ignorance.**

In the misuse of another human being, whom he or she manipulates through guilt and shame, the addict succeeds many times in draining the life force from those he or she seeks to hold fast through manipulation and control.

It is a sad testimony to our society that because our hearts have been broken by those we love, we are so fearful of abandonment that we tie and bind those we supposedly "love" to us with steel controls that imprison their very being. Like caged wild creatures, we are dying inside with secret desperation and the longing to be free to discover our purpose, our meaning in life.

We no longer know what it means to love. We rule through guilt and fear because it is the only way we know.

All this is done in the name of love; however, it is a perversion of love, one that is utterly destructive. It is the antithesis of love. It is complete denial. Addicts are masters at maintaining their will, the Iron Will of Ignorance.

At one of my cancer support groups, we polled the members and, out of thirty-five people, almost every one was either married to or significantly bonded to a key family member who was an addict.

I do not know if any statistics have been taken on the correlation between alcoholism/addiction and cancer, but I have found it to be a prevalent theme.

Addicts draw the life out of people by *denying their feelings*. Anyone who has lived with an addict knows the hopelessness of dealing with the Iron Will of Ignorance manifested on a daily basis. It is a losing battle, and since the addict's will is without conscience and seeks only to isolate and gratify itself, a feeling person living with such a personality will not last long. You will find your belief in yourself dwindling, your self-esteem shattered and your personal power drained and emptied. The addict needs this to survive. He is like a many-armed octopus, psychically covered with sucker shoots that latch onto your body's energy, your finances, your well-being. You will find your health, prosperity, livelihood, indeed, your sanity slowly ebb away to the all encompassing octopus, whose needs can never be satiated or gratified.

Sounds pretty devastating, does it not? It is. The destructiveness of this personality cannot be underestimated. The sad part of it is, within himself, the addict lives in darkness and misery. He is totally absorbed in the drama of his own life and cannot truly feel for another human being.

Relationships with the addictive personality are sealed with a common bond of anger and guilt. Since the addict is in denial of his own rage, he rules with an iron hand. He is a master at provoking pity and instills guilt in those he seeks to control.

How did this all come about?

Though I do not have the opportunity in this book to delve deeply into the problem of addiction (it would take a book in itself), I have made some interesting observations in the course of my work that might be of importance to you. For an in depth look at addiction, read *Healing the Shame that Binds You* by John Bradshaw.

The Demonic Bond

As sensitive children, dependent upon the adults in our lives for our very survival, we experienced a rejection of our true, feeling selves by adults who, through their own conditioning, were incapable of giving us unconditional love. The experience of being drawn in love toward the powerful parent and then rejected was a truly terrifying experience. We never knew what mood the critical parent would project, so our experience was one of constant anxiety accompanied by denied rage, over-whelming guilt and shame. This "push me, pull me" type of relationship left us unable to bond with the rejecting parent. As a result, we became divided within our own selves, reenacting the vulnerability/rejection syndrome of childhood by internal-izing the offending parent.

The "push me/pull me" syndrome bonded us in an abusive, unhealthy way to the controlling parent. A bond was formed between the insecure, emotionally vacillating parent and our-selves that was not an actual bond, but a bondage.

The essence of this demonic bond between parent and child is:

"I'll provide for you materially and financially (take care of you)

if

you'll never leave me (be free to have a life)."

I call this a demonic bondage because it is truly the enslave-ment of the weaker human being, who, as a little child, had no choice for survival other than to accept the terms of this demonic pact.

In true Mephistophilian fashion, the parent need never have to admit the truth of growing older (denial); while the child can never be free to grow up.

The insecure parent is assured against abandonment while the child physically grows older. Meanwhile, the child's emotional maturity remains arrested at an early age, usually adolescence. As an adult, the frightened child within cannot emotionally relate in male/female relationships. There is a thwarted sexuality, a confused sexual identity, at the core of every addict. Only alcohol or drugs can dull the pain of this enslavement, which is essentially the loss of the child's soul.

Birth of an Addict

As an adult, then, the addict repeats this push/pull bondage in his adult relationships. He is divided, therefore he is incapable of true intimacy or emotional bonding. As he or she moves forward into feeling and bonding with the opposite sex, the internalized parent within rushes forward like an angry demon to seize control of the vulnerable child. This is an experience of utter abandonment and rejection for the partner of the addict. It is a direct reenactment of the childhood experience of the addict.

A new demonic bond is formed, this time, between addict and partner. As the confused partner seeks to merge with the addict, he or she reaches a certain point, only to be emotionally distanced just at the point of true emotional connection. This is a devastating experience, especially since the addict in an instant performs an almost Jekyll-and-Hyde transformation from vulnerability to anger and attack. The partner, uninformed and innocent, may feel responsible for the addict's rage and becomes tied to the addictive personality through overwhelming feelings of guilt and inadequacy.

Thus, a new demonic bond, in a relationship of anger and guilt, is sealed once again.

The experience of addiction is one of returning time and time again to receive what we need from a source and never quite acquiring it. So we return again and again, searching to have our needs met, only to be taken halfway there and abandoned.

This is a way of life for the addictive personality. It is the only life he knows.

I hope I have not frightened you by the words I have used in describing the problem of addiction. Perhaps you think that words like demon are extreme, but I can assure you they are not. In viewing, through my work and life experience, the abject suffering of humanity in today's society, it is only fitting and proper that we view this affliction with the attention and gravity it deserves in order for it to be fully understood.

Alcoholism and addiction are rampant in today's society. In observing the devastating and tragic consequences of relationship with this type of individual, the only way we can empower ourselves and heal our lives is through understanding the core issues inherent in this personality.

The Hedonistic Mask

Since this personality lives in denial of truth, any type of behavior is possible. Hedonistic behavior, promiscuity, criminal acting out, lies, deceit, the need to live in secrecy and denial— all are commonplace in the life of the addictive personality. Though the addict suffers intensely because of his own actions, he is at the mercy of himself and doomed to repeat them if he does not reach out for help in order to change.

In the course of my work, I employ techniques of meditation and relaxation to help people tune in to their inner selves. In observing the faces of those suffering the problem of addiction while in repose, I have noticed a curious thing. Upon the composed features of the addict's face there is an overlay of energy that looks like a smile. Though the face may be suffering, superimposed upon the features is a smile I have come to call the hedonistic mask.

This "smile" is not pleasant or joyous; it is sinister and mocking.

I have found it to be a negative part of the personality that undermines faith, love and belief. It is like an energy, or force that acts as a shield or barrier to the authentic self. In exploring this concept further, it is my feeling that the path of God, love, faith and spiritual belief is the only "cure," or healing for the addictive personality.

Trapped within the addict is a lost, frightened, suffering, innocent child. The vulnerability and sweetness of this imprisoned being is tragic to behold.

Those of us who have lived with this personality know the pain of viewing the suffering within this personality, the self-destructiveness, and our own futile desire to move forward in the need to help and love, only to be rejected and attacked by the full fury of the enraged internalized parent that guards and controls the vulnerable, innocent being. That enraged internalized parent can take any number of forms—critic, ego, demon of fear, anger, guilt and shame. Yes, it is truly as if more than one personality is housed within the body of this destructive, suffering human being.

What can those of us who love these people do most to help?

Help and Healing

First of all, we can **let go** of the need to help and allow the addictive personality to be responsible for his or her own life. As long as this personality can manipulate someone else to bear responsibility for them, they will never need to change.

We can then seek help for our own damaged self-esteem and, in many cases, health, livelihood, finances, and otherwise battered lives.

The healing of the addictive personality is in **taking on the responsibility of his or her own life, in recognizing the need to change, and in allowing God, truth, light and love to enter and heal.**

There are wonderful rehabilitation centers and twelve-step programs that are becoming an active and essential part of our society. If you are living with an addict and are becoming inwardly confused, desperate and hopeless, and are fortunate enough to read these lines, *get help for yourself.* Pick up the phone, call a friend, a therapist. Get information on recovery for your own wounded being. Shift the focus of your life away from the other person and onto your own self.

Take care of yourself. Only then can we seek to help, by example, anyone else.

Those of us who abdicated our responsibility for our own happiness and took on the impossible task of trying to fix another person must look at our own issues. What hook are we on?

This "hook" manifests in an actual spot of pain within our own body, in the stomach area. Perhaps we have lived with this painful sensation so long we are not even aware of it. It is a place in the stomach that becomes an area of pain and suffering.

This feeling, I have discovered, is nothing more than the need to emotionally bond in love with another human being. It is a feeling that goes back to infancy in our need for love, caring, emotional nurturing and actual physical sustenance.

When we are suffering from this painful physical sensation, we can actually help ourselves assist in our own healing by giving ourselves the attention, love and nurturing we require; in essence, we can bond in love with ourselves and fulfill our own physical and emotional needs.

Dr. M. Halpern has written about "attachment hunger" in his *How to Break Your Addiction to a Person*. This book explores addiction in love relationships and I highly recommend it.

I would like to conclude this chapter with a letter written by a dear man suffering from alcoholism and dying of cancer. He wrote this letter to his now deceased mother and father:

Dear Mr. and Mrs.—,

Biologically, you are my mother and father, but there is an awful lot more than conception and birth to being one's Mom and Dad.

Mom and Dad are supposed to be the two most important people in a young person's life. Unfortunately, except for the fact that you provided me so well with the material things in life, I really didn't even know who you were. There was always too much going on in your lives to afford you the time—if you wanted it—to be more than a disciplinarian as far as I was concerned.

Also, unfortunately—and this time my Family paid the price—I didn't realize until much later that you both were alcoholics. By then, I had made myself one, too. Thus, I not only didn't know you, but I was introduced to a life-style that perpetuated itself in me, and caused me to inflict a lot of pain and grief. I simply wasn't strong enough on my own to do otherwise.

I heard you were great and generous people. I sure wish I had known you better. You—as I—were incapable of showing love. If you were as great and generous as you were, there must have been a lot of love there somewhere. As I look back, it would have been nice to share it with you.

You hold the keys to unlocking the prison within yourself that guards you from joy, love, self-esteem and happiness. In the violence and suffering of today's afflicted society, empowerment of the human individual is the only answer. Make the motivation of love for yourself propel you forward in the momentum it takes to heal your life. In every choice, ask yourself this question, "Will this choice help heal the wounded being within myself?" This question will help you determine the powerful choices that will create a loving, meaningful existence for you and those you love.

Do not let fear hold you back. Step forward. You are important! God loves and forgives all unconditionally. The actions you take to heal your own life will assist in the healing of all of humanity. Do not despair or give in to hopelessness, but push forward. I am rooting for you! Go forth in peace, and remember the words of Winston Churchill: *"Never, never, never, never, never give up!"*

Exercise: Healing the Agony of Rejection— Emotional Bonding and Rebirthing

1) Heat up a glass of warm milk. You may consume this milk either in a glass, or you may actually pour it into a baby's bottle and relive the experience of feeding and receiving in a positive and loving way.

2) As the warm milk flows down into your body, close your eyes and feel the warmth and nurturing. Place your hands on the painful area and imagine a healing warmth and energy flowing from your own hands into your body, offering relief and affection. You may even wrap yourself in a quilt or blanket and keep your arms around your own body, hugging yourself in a gesture of love and caring.

3) Visualize yourself as a tiny infant, being held in your own loving, nurturing arms, being rocked and comforted, physically nourished and satisfied. You are loving yourself, filling all your needs, and giving yourself the love and nurturing you need for peace and happiness. You are fully capable of giving this to yourself, of healing your own wounded being.

You can actually feel the healing flowing through you, the light, the love, the healing energy. There is no need for pain and suffering. You are lovable, huggable, believable, wonderful. You are a sweet and innocent being who deserves the most wonderful life imaginable, a child of God whose first loyalty is to your authentic, powerful self. Feel the pain dissolve in the powerful energy of divine love and healing. There is no force greater than that of love in its purest form. *You deserve* to receive this love; feel yourself *opening* to receive it in every cell of your body. You are joy, love, and inner peace. This is *who you are*. You are no longer lost in the illusion of human suffering, but are returning to that love within, the beauty, the wonder, the peace. All is well in your world.

Exercise for Morning Anxiety:

Be aware of the fear and anxiety. Pay attention to your breathing. Focus your attention on drawing in the sacred breath of life to your heart center. Feel the energy fill your heart. Open to the feeling.

You can actually feel a space beginning to open in your heart as the energy flows freely through you. Put your arms around yourself and experience a sense of love for the being that is you.

Say aloud, "I love you and I accept you exactly as you are, and I am taking care of you!"

Feel yourself opening in trust to the new day.

You may experience this prayer as well, which I composed during the course of my life and which connects me each morning in peace and love to the Creator.

My Prayer

Dear Lord, please protect and guide my life. Surround me with your light and protect and guide those I love. Shine your light on my path and give me the courage to go through the doors you open for me. Dear Lord, give me peace of mind. Thank you, Lord, for my many blessings. Amen.

By the time you take your bath or shower you will be feeling a sense of hope and joy flow through you as you begin your day. Make this day one of healing, love and joy!

Affirmations:

Many people in today's afflicted society experience turmoil and anxiety as the sun begins to set and night approaches. Some experience a burning in the stomach area as the fear sets in. I have developed a series of affirmations to heal the anxiety and to open to a sense of reverence and serenity as we say good-bye to the day and welcome the approaching evening.

You may light a candle as you turn inward with reverence, opening yourself to receive love and healing.

Five o'clock Prayers

- I joyously release this day.
- I feel gratitude for my many blessings.
- I communicate a feeling of love to my body.
- I hereby release the need for suffering.
- I feel God's love and light releasing me and filling me up.
- I feel the glow of the setting sun's warmth flow through me as I open to God's grace.
- With gratitude and peace, I prepare for my evening.
- I feel the beauty and love within me and give thanks to myself, and to all those I love and hold dearly, and to the sacred planet upon which I live.
- I love myself.
- All is in divine order.
- All is well in my world.
- I let go of the past and assume responsibility for my sacred being.
- I am Free—

12

*Two monks were walking on the road when they
passed a beautiful woman trying to cross a spot that
was filled with water. Without hesitation, one of the
monks picked the woman up and carried her across
the road. Horrified, the other monk went on and on
about how his friend had broken the rules by having
contact with a woman. Nonplussed, the monk
replied, "I put the woman down a mile back down the
road, but you're still carrying her."*

—Spiritual story

There may be guilt when there is too much virtue.

—B. PASCAL, *Pensées*

The guilty flee when no man pursueth.

—BIBLE, Prov. 28:1

The Hidden
Saboteur—Guilt

As much as I would like to leave this chapter out, I would be
remiss in my duty to you if I didn't say a few important things
about guilt. You see, I am like anyone else—I don't like to deal
with guilt!

Dr. Joan Borysenko has written an excellent volume on
guilt, entitled *Guilt is the Teacher, Love is the Lesson,* and I highly
recommend it to everyone.

Guilt is the most unconscious and destructive force imaginable within a human being. It is lethal, because it is so painful

that most of us block it out so that we do not feel it at all. Yet it exists within us, like a hidden saboteur, destroying our self-esteem, poisoning our relationships, and causing us to make destructive choices against our selves.

There has not been one person I've worked with in Self-Healing who did not deny the presence of guilt feelings. Yet, as our work progressed, the guilt unearthed was all-pervasive and shocking in its severity.

The illness of cancer is like a giant guilt machine you can step into if your buried guilt and shame have reached an intolerable level of toxicity. Beneath the surface of the anger and resentment lies a bedrock of buried guilt.

It is the same with anxiety attacks. Beneath the free floating panic is a tidal wave of guilt. If you can get in touch with it and allow yourself to cry, you will find the fear dissolving into relief.

A Lesson in Guilt: The Girl on the Railroad Tracks

The first time I had cancer, I had to rally all the forces within myself to find the will power to overcome my tremendous fear and survive. As I looked within, a visualization would come forth of a part of me that wanted to "throw itself on the railroad tracks and die."

This was a terrifying realization! There was actually a part of me that wanted to die!

As I fought for my life, this hidden part of me would surface in that bizarre imagery of railroad tracks and death. This remained a mystery I would try to delve into, but, try as I might, I just couldn't pierce through the veil to feel the pain that could heal me.

It was only many years later, after I had started Self-Healing, that the universe provided just the right set of circumstances to trigger the key to a buried part of myself, and a childhood trauma revealed itself to me in a shocking moment of clarity and realization. I remembered a scene from the past when I was five years old. The peace and stillness of morning was shattered by the appearance of a policeman at the front door. I remember the pain and shock on my mother's face as the policeman told her that my father had had a serious accident. The terrible details were explained to her. While running for the train, my father had fallen, been dragged and then been thrown on the railroad tracks by the departing train.

I remember the terror I felt at visiting my father and witnessing him in pain in a hospital bed. I bit my lips to hold back the tears. My all-powerful father cut down by a near-fatal accident!

Though he fully recovered, somehow I had internalized the responsibility for my father's accident. Somehow I could have prevented it; somehow it was all my fault.

I must say here that no one blamed me for the accident. Up until the moment I "realized" and *felt* the pain of my internalized guilt, I hadn't known for a moment that I actually had blamed myself for my father's accident! This was an absolutely stunning realization!

I know now that children feel responsible to heal the pain in the lives of the powerful adults they turn to for the love they need to survive. This is a simple fact. Why it is so, I don't know. It just is. Children willingly carry the burden of guilt for the adults in their lives. Most of this burden is assumed unconsciously, and it ties us in unhealthy bonds of guilt to parental figures.

Have you ever felt tears spring to your eyes when thinking about your mother or father? Many times this is a symptom of unhealthy feelings of guilt attached to the parent that freezes us emotionally and makes it impossible to go forward in life on an emotional level.

Though I remembered my father's accident intellectually, I was not able to connect with the pain and guilt and heal. Cancer helped me release the internalized guilt and shame of a lifetime. That is part of the reason why cancer was such a great gift to me. That guilt and shame were costing me my life.

Because of the realization and release of my own buried guilt, I am able to focus in on the pain of those who come to me for help and healing. I know now that these emotional blocks become stored up in our bodies as serious illness.

The worst part about guilt is that it is usually so painful that we deny it. It then becomes an unconscious saboteur, causing us to make unhealthy choices that reflect our lack of self-esteem. Guilt paralyzes us from acting on our own behalf. We simply become the helpless pawns of others, because we are held captive within ourselves by an unknown force that sabotages our actions for the good through feelings of shame and unworthiness. It is as if we are held hostage by an unhealthy part of our own selves.

Since this process is usually unconscious, it is our personal responsibility to ourselves to seek the help we need to ferret out these unhealthy feelings and release them into love and light. Only then can we become empowered individuals, free to make the healthy, enlightened choices that create meaningful, happy lives.

Do you remember the wonderful man I spoke about earlier, the one who worked at healing his angry inner child named Chuckie? As the path of this man's work progressed, he developed a pain in his left arm and elbow. He began to have anxiety attacks, fearing a possible heart attack.

We approached the problem by attempting to discover what this man's body was trying to communicate to him in order to assist in his inner healing. This positive approached allayed his feelings of panic and fear. Through relaxation, meditation, and visualization we probed the blockage in his arm and interpreted his body's message.

He remembered an autumn day as a teenager when he was asked to rake leaves. His mother had asked him earlier to begin raking, but he had waited a few minutes while his father assumed the job. After awhile, he took the rake from his father and was grudgingly finishing the work when his mother ran screaming from the house that his father had had a heart attack. In the ensuing panic, his mother blamed him for his father's heart attack.

My client could hardly remember clearly the events that followed. He recounted the hazy blur of his father's funeral and a feeling of guilt and anguish that had never left him. Although he had been in recovery for alcohol abuse for many years, this event had never surfaced on a feeling level of any significance.

We worked together to dig out all the pain on a feeling level—especially on forgiveness and guilt release. My client realized he felt *too guilty to live.*

He had to forgive himself and give himself *permission to live.* With the passage of time, unconditional love, forgiveness and understanding allowed this man to heal his anxiety attacks, cancer, and, in his eventual realization of his great fear of love, the roots of alcoholism.

I have helped many people to realize that unconscious guilt toward a loved one was actually forcing them to obey an unconscious death wish in the form of cancer or substance abuse. I have seen people ill with cancer realize their feelings that deceased family members were calling them "to the other side." These people needed to give themselves conscious *permission to go on in life and live.* These feelings are very, very common and very human. Only when denied do they have the power to hurt and destroy us.

In conscious realization of truth, there is always healing. It is an unfortunate human tendency to resist and battle the things that afford us the most good. Healing takes courage and conscious effort to overcome tremendous resistance. Remember, the truth always sets us free.

I am so happy this chapter is finished! Guilt feelings are hypnotic; they turn our attention away from the present moment back to a focus in the past, a barricade to love and intimacy that must be disassembled brick by brick until it is gone and we are free!

Shift your focus back to now, to yourself, and own your freedom to have joy, love, peace and health. You deserve it, you are worthy, and you are so loved!

Exercise: How to move through and out of an anxiety attack

Feel the pressure building within you, the tremendous free-floating fear. Go with the feeling, try to flow beneath the fear. What has happened to cause you to feel trapped by guilt? You are suffocating—come up for air! Allow the tears to flow freely. Feel the tension releasing throughout your body. Feel free to cry. Put your arms around yourself and say, "I love you and I accept you exactly as you are, and I am taking care of you."

Look at yourself in the mirror. Say aloud once again, "I love you."

Write your feelings in your journal. What have you just learned about yourself?

Take a bath or a shower. The water will help your body to feel solid and strong.

Affirmations

ᴇ᙭ I am worthy to receive my good.

ᴇ᙭ I am opening to receive my good from others.

ᴇ᙭ I am good enough.

ᴇ᙭ I give myself permission to enjoy my life.

ᴇ᙭ I release the need for illness and pain to receive the attention, recognition and love I need and deserve in my life.

ᴇ᙭ I open joyfully to receive these gifts.

ᴇ᙭ I release my need for pain and suffering.

ᴇ᙭ I release the guilt and fear that have held me back and joyfully embrace the flow of life and go with it to my great good.

- All the experiences within my body and life exist to teach me something valuable about myself.

- I handle the experiences with gratitude and use the wisdom I have to direct my life in divine right order.

- All is well in my world.

REVOLUTION

Angela Passidomo Trafford

There was a time
In Life
When I struggled to go
Up up up
But, really, I was headed
Down down down

Then
I fought hard
And despaired
At going
Down down down
But really
I was buoying
Up up up

For you see
I had been taught
To view
The world upside down
Therefore I believed
That down was up
And up was down
And nowhere I trod was steady ground
Then I took
The world in
My hands
And made
It stand still
So that I could
Get my balance
After my
Head cleared
I steadied my heart
And walked
With courage
And dread
Straight ahead

PALOMA BLANCA

Hans Bouwens

When the sun shines on the mountain
And the night is on the run
It's a new day
It's a new way
And I fly up to the sun

(Refrain)
Una Paloma Blanca
I'm just a bird in the sky
Una Paloma Blanca
Over the mountains I fly
No one can take my freedom away

I can feel the morning sunlight
I can smell the newborn hay
I can hear God's voices calling
From my golden skylight way

(Refrain)

Once I had my share of losing
Once they locked me on a chain
Yes they tried to break my power
Oh, I still can feel the pain—

(Refrain)

No one can take my freedom away!
Yes! No one can take my freedom away!

13

We are always getting ready to live, but never living.

—Ralph Waldo Emerson

The soul alone raises us to nobility.

—Seneca, *Epistles*

There are times when all the world's asleep
The questions run so deep
For such a simple man.
Won't you please—
I know it sounds absurd—
Please tell me who I am?

—Supertramp, "The Rational Song"

Fortune favors those who dare.

—Virgil

Free to Be Who You Are: Release of Conditioning

Five years ago, when I received those two phone calls stating, first, that I had lost the custody of my children, and second, that I had a recurrence of cancer, I was so overwhelmed with pain that I literally could not stand to be in my own body.

There was no escape from the intensity of a suffering so total; all I had strength left to do was to fall to my knees on my living room floor and beg for God's mercy and forgiveness.

From the depths of my being, I cried out to God for help. There was nowhere else to go, nothing else to do, no one else to turn to: *this was it*.

I asked God to forgive me for the way I had lived my life. I admitted that I did not know how to live, and that the way I was living my life was wrong, though I had no idea how this was so. It had all led to illness and tragedy; even my intellectual mind had to admit that *I was wrong*.

I then **let go of my life to God**.

I asked God to take my life and show me how to live. There was no one else to turn to; my trust in the people I loved was shattered. No one I knew of was truly happy or had the answers for me. My cry to God was wrenched from the depths of my soul.

I then opened my eyes and looked to life itself for guidance and information. What followed was a child-like state of absolute humility, humbleness, and innocence. Much to my amazement, this state of consciousness felt good! It was a relief, a relief from having to know it all. I did not know it then, but this was the transformation of my ego.

I realized my former state of mind had been an intolerable strain and burden, yet, I had not been able to see or admit this to myself. My new perception of reality brought me into *total awareness*. There was an instant sense of comfort and peace. From that moment on, my life changed. From that moment on, I have had the blessings of one miracle after another.

That moment was, in actuality, a sudden death. I died to the old way of being. Then God resurrected me with light and love, and enfolded my being and my life in joy and grace. His beloved daughter had returned home! A celebration was in order, a celebration of life.

I looked at the past, and had an astounding realization. It was all ashes, an illusion of suffering.

This was a most amazing awareness: the past was an illusion of pain and suffering, an illusion of my own creation. It was a true spiritual awakening.

Have you ever had a horrible nightmare that seemed real, and then you were so relieved and happy to wake up? Well, this was somewhat like the nature of my experience; as close as human words can come to describing an absolutely instantaneous revolution of consciousness.

I truly gave over my life to God at that point and submitted. The Iron Will of Ignorance submitted to the Divine Will of God. In one fell swoop, the conditioning of the past, the family, the school, the society, was gone. The human being was born.

How joyful I have become since that time! God's love healed all my wounds and salved my shattered being. From the ruins emerged a sweet, vulnerable, innocent spiritual child, who opened her eyes in wonder at the beautiful world that surrounded her. This being was whole and complete. She was not renewed, she had always been new! Her purity of heart and feeling had been imprisoned in a casket of stone. Now, her innocence and purity shone radiantly upon the world in which she lived. All was anew. She walked the earth joyful, ageless, pure and strong, in the divine light of truth. She need not fear. Her path was now lit at every step for her. She felt within and around her at all times the divine presence of God. This divine presence was a shield and a sword, a comfort and a peace, an inner knowing of being blessed and unconditionally, divinely loved.

All her trust was there, untarnished by experience. She was real, her body resurrected and restored. The words of Jesus come to mind: "Lest ye like little children be, ye cannot know the kingdom of heaven."

My dear friends, only in the release of conditioning can we be real. Only in the release of conditioning can we grasp reality and come into total awareness of *being*. A conditioned mind is a dead mind. We must look to the *now* for life and heavenly release from the past.

Looking to the *now* involves the choice to do so. The choice to pay attention in the here and now. The choice to care, to feel, to be. This choice, the choice *to be*, entails assuming the responsibility for one's life.

In the Assuming of this Responsibility Lies Total Freedom.
Total Responsibility = Total Freedom

The realization of this truth is the acceptance of what seems to be a paradox. It is a genuine turning point.

Personal Power

Luck is not chance
It is toil
Fortune's expensive smile
Is earned.

—Emily Dickinson

In the decision to release all conditioning and go forward into life itself, a human being becomes empowered. Life itself reaches out to support the individual in every way possible. This soon becomes apparent and gives each moment an air of magic and mystery. Coincidences occur in your favor; there is a persistent feeling of being loved and supported; one feels "lucky," seemingly for no reason at all.

Many of us had this feeling in childhood—the acceptance, humor and spontaneity, the bounding forth into life with confidence and trust. Little children are devoid of ego, and so they are close to God and their true divine nature. They seem to have no trouble deciding what to do, or what they want. If you observe them closely, they are not in thought, they are alive in the present moment and at peace when at rest. Little children are happy at play and move easily through emotions—anger, joy, laughter, tears. They are free and alive. How adults envy children their laughter and joy!

In the release of the conditioned mind, a new state of consciousness evolves. There is emotional response, honesty of communication, a lack of fear in expressing feelings and truth. A human being is alive and empowered.

One lives the truth of the affirmation:

☞ *As I love and support myself, so does God and the universe support me.*

Recently I was honored to be a presenter at the International Love and Health Congress sponsored by the University of Southern Connecticut in New Haven, Connecticut. The experience of love and sharing proved to be a truly transformational experience for all participants.

A question was asked by a member of the audience, "Can the mind release all conditioning spontaneously, in one moment of time?"

The answer is yes, it is indeed possible, if the desire and intention is great enough, sincere enough, and all pervasive. Again, the Upanishadic scriptures come to mind: if the need is great enough, "If you want the truth as badly as a drowning man wants air, then you will realize it in a split second."

I know this is possible, because this was my experience.

The logical mind seeks explanations for the unspeakable. This is only fitting and appropriate, because it gives us a sense of inner balance. In my quest to understand and realize some of my experience, I came across a book called *Transformed by the Light,* by Dr. Melvin Morse. In the chapter entitled "The Glow of God," Morse states that he believes human beings have two nervous systems, each guided by separate portions of the brain. The left side is the conventional biochemical nervous system regulating motor and sensory abilities. He then defines the right half of what he calls the "dual nervous system:"

> The other [nervous system] is a subtle, electromagnetic nervous system which is responsible for healing bone breaks, regeneration of body tissue, and the psychosomatic linkages between the brain and body.
>
> It also accounts for our paranormal abilities, things such as telepathy, precognition, and out-of-body experiences. This is the silent person, the inner conscience, the part of us that communicates with God.

It is within this silent second brain—the circuit boards of mysticism—that we can understand the nature of the near-death experience. When the brain dies and input from the biochemical nervous system ceases, this area of the right temporal lobe turns on, usually for the first time in our lives. It allows us to receive a wonderful and loving light, which one patient called "the glow of God."

Those who recover from nearly dying are transformed by this light. They understand that their lives have purpose and meaning, usually involving love of family and mankind in general. They reactivate dormant areas of their brain and discover newly-born abilities, both of the paranormal and intuitive variety. They become happy people with hobbies and intellectual pursuits. They spend time alone in meditation. They spend more time in community affairs and helping professions than the "ordinary" population.

Dr. Morse refers to the right temporal lobe as the "seat of the soul."

I believe this to be a possible scientific "explanation" for the instantaneous release-of-conditioning/rebirth experience that transforms a person not only psychically and spiritually, but physiologically as well. It is, in essence, spontaneous healing.

It is well known in spiritual literature that, as the spiritual energy, or kundalini energy, rises in the human being, the body itself expands and transforms in order to receive and transmute this sacred energy of love and light.

Whether conditioning is released instantaneously, or, in most cases, over the course of time, it is a process that requires inner work, attention and ardent motivation.

In the release of conditioning, we find ourselves! The glory of it is that, as we let go of all the pain and suffering of the past, as we forgive everyone and everything, we then return to that blissful consciousness of peace and unconditional love. We are illuminated and awakened to who we are.

It is our challenge as human beings to pierce through the layers of delusion through which we wander without meaning, until the intensity of our purpose burns through the mists of illusion and we discover reality.

This is the heroic challenge we must embrace with all our hearts and minds, the holy grail to which we must aspire, for the reward is nothing less than our authentic being.

Meditation: Recovering Creative Power

Let us journey together in this simple meditation back to the eternal source of light within, and remember that Light and Love is who we are.

Take a deep breath, closing your eyes. . . . Allow the sacred breath of life to flow into your heart center, filling your heart with feelings of love and peace. Feel the movement of energy within your heart, expanding and uplifting you. . .

Visualize yourself as you are right now. . . . Now visualize a radiant, blissful white light within yourself. This light is filled with the bliss of unconditional love. Feel the light within. . . . This love is who you are! Flow without fear into the love. Let the flow of light wash away any relationships you are now involved in. . . . Feel yourself journeying back through time. Visualize the faces of your loved ones and travel beyond them. . . . Slip back into the light until you can visualize yourself as a little child. . . . Allow yourself to feel the soul connection to this beautiful little being that is you. . . . View the faces of your mother and father. . . . Allow the feelings, both negative and positive. . . . Feel the sorrow and anger melt away into the healing balm of forgiveness. . . . Feel the love. . . . Let go of your parents as you slip back into the warm radiant energy. . . . You are letting go, but it is easier now, it feels so wonderful to bathe freely in the light and let go to the flow. . . . You are visualizing your infant self now. . . . Connect with the pure and beautiful newborn soul that is you. . . . Shower feelings of love and nurturing on the newborn child. Celebrate your birth. It took courage to be born! Bless the tiny, sacred being, and feel yourself letting go once again. . . .

You are a seed now, a seed of light and creative energy. . . . You are a dream in the mind of the creator, waiting to be born. . . . Move freely in the warm energy of love. You are creation itself, all powerful! . . .

Be who you are. Flow forth in your love and create the life that is worthy of you. . . . Allow your sacred intention to manifest on the earth plane. Remember who you are, a beloved child of God. . . .

Surface once again into consciousness, feeling empowered by the peace within yourself. Bring this sense of peace into your day and into the rest of your life.

Exercise:

Think of a negative "doing" that has become a pattern.

Example: Being critical and unsupportive of yourself.

Now, pratice "not doing" that pattern. Let it go and practice a pattern of giving yourself a lot of love and support. Be aware of the difference in how you feel about youself. Practice for one week.

Which "doing" is your preference? Write your new awareness in your journal. Once you take steps to make changes in yourself through choice and awareness, you will see that *change is possible*. It is a process.

Affirmations:

- I let go of the misery of the past.
- I let go of my belief that life cannot be wonderful and joyful.
- I realize this is a false belief based on the painful experiences of childhood.
- I open to the belief that life is wonderful and good, and I am ready and open to receive my good.
- I am grateful for my many blessings.
- All is well in my world.

Acquiring personal power is synonymous with integrity and living in the light of truth. I have evolved some beautiful affirmations to assist in the development of this state of awareness.

In the recitation of these affirmations, you will find your state of mind turning toward the positive. You will actually experience a shift in consciousness from negative to positive. By choosing to incorporate truth, love and courage in your actions, you therefore empower yourself in life. By choosing to act in this right manner, you are uplifting yourself into a higher mode of being. Your life takes on the integrity of a higher order, truly the path of the hero.

- God's love is flowing through me, giving me the courage to act and speak my truth.
- There is nothing to fear. I am safe.
- God is speaking through me.
- The words I say are right and appropriate.
- God is acting through me.
- My actions are in accord with God's will.
- My life is divinely guided and protected.
- I feel the strength of God's love as a power and an energy.
- I now go forth with courage to claim my good.
- As I love and support myself, so does God and the Universe support me.
- God's will is my will.
- I am on my path in life.
- All the help I need is here for me.
- I am safe.

14

Finding out what love is means more to me
than bread or water.

Now, with a new attitude, a new spirit, a new life, I
will place no unwarranted stress on this holy crucible
of life that is my body on this earth. This is the pledge
I make to myself. Never again will I let anything, or
anyone, drag me down into suffering.
Each day is too sacred to waste.

—From my journal, the first time I had cancer.

Slowing Down and *Paying Attention*

Keeping a Journal

It is amazing what a true release it is to record your feelings in your own private journal. The actual experience of viewing your own feelings written in black and white by your own hand is to be aware of reality. It gives your feelings validity. Since the path to health is through the feeling self, we must gain access to ourselves in order to find out what our true feelings are. When you see your own private reflections down on paper, you are able to learn more about the mysterious puzzle that is you. As time goes on and your journal gathers momentum, you can look back and discern patterns that are destructive and gain information about healing these patterns.

How often my own words have come back to me as healing reminders to assist me in going forward consciously along my path in life! Through the validation of my feelings, I am able to take positive action to ensure my values and priorities. Being able to take affirmative action on my own behalf gives me self-esteem. This is truly what it means to love yourself.

When I first started a journal many years ago, I wrote these words, "Do I really have something to say, or am I just going mad staring at my own reflection?"

How different I am today! Back then, I was lost in the delusion of my life, a powerless victim.

When I had cancer the first time, I wrote in my journal that I was fighting "for the freedom to have faith—to hope for the best." I had to battle through the negativity permeating the oncology ward. It was a battle, but I took it on, I did it, and I won! If I could accomplish this, I who was so victimized, so passive, there is no doubt in my mind that you can have success as well. Once you find your true path in life, there is no telling what miracles await you. I live this principle and I know it works.

All it takes is some faith in ourselves and some effort to bring these riches to the surface. Love brings it all to life. With love in the heart, a person can take on any challenge, and oftentimes succeed! This is my upbeat message for today. There is hope, if you have the courage to place your faith in life. Experience the pain, because it is part of being alive. Sorry, but the acceptance of the total package is what brings it all together. In the absence of conflict, love can survive; happiness exists if we allow it. We are always striving for something more, so we miss out on the beauty of what is.

These words I wrote in my journal many years ago, the first time I had cancer.

You can feel the courage and hope that shines forth from these words. And this was just at the beginning! How happy I am that I recorded my journey of life; the agony and ecstasy of my struggles is so interesting and moving to me! It makes me feel good about myself. And now it may be helping you as well, and that makes me feel even better!

Since then I have accepted the absolute fact that life itself is a challenge that we must heroically take on to become powerful, authentic, joyful human beings. In conquering the innermost battle within ourselves, in healing the division between heart and mind, we become whole human beings, capable of unconditional love. We then transform into a force that directly acts as a positive force of transformation upon all those whom we encounter in our lives.

When I ask each person I work with to keep a journal, inevitably I receive the same reply. "Someone might find it!" or, "I hate to have to write down all my feelings. I hate having to feel at all!"

These comments help us start to take an honest look at our lives. Why have we no privacy or sacred space for ourselves? Why are we not honoring ourselves? What feelings are we denying? Why don't we want to face our true feelings about ourselves and our relationships? Why are we hiding from the truth?

We then realize that facing the truth of our feelings gives us a responsibility to ourselves to act on our own behalf. And this is where we falter.

We must have faith in life itself to assist us on our divine journey. *We must believe in what we feel.*

The journal is an excellent tool to get us in touch with what these feelings are.

The Art of Listening

Most people are too busy thinking or wondering what they are going to say next to listen to anyone else. In actuality, most of us are in rebellion; we made a conscious choice long ago *not to listen.* I myself was once this way. It was shocking for me to realize that I had lost respect for the human beings who surrounded me, and that I had lost my faith in life itself to reveal answers to me. I was busy, as most of us are, proving myself *right.*

I was an encapsulated missile of fear and ignorance hurtling chaotically through life. I never paused to actually listen and receive information from anyone or anything. I had, as a child, realized the hypocrisy of many adults who enjoyed giving advice to others, advice they would never take themselves! Therefore, unbeknownst to me, my ears were boarded up; my inner intelligence was buried beneath layers of anger, guilt, shame and fear. I was lost!

In point of fact, since my heart has opened, I have noticed this tendency in many of my fellow human beings. They are too entrapped within thought and lack the trust and awareness necessary to open up and listen.

Listening requires attention. You must be centered in a place of humility and honestly ask the universe for answers. Prayer is one way of asking God and the universe for help and answers. We must pray, believing that help is forthcoming, and be humble enough to pay attention moment by moment to the world around us in order to receive those answers. We must have courage enough to attempt to emerge from the mired concrete we have settled into through our addiction to security—and risk a swim in the flow of life itself.

Swimming in the flow of life is being in awareness. It is being alive. It means listening to another's feelings and honoring them. It means pausing to reflect inwardly with humbleness and the spirit of honest inquiry. It means meditation; it means learning what a meditative life is all about, and it means having the courage to live it.

Listening means paying attention with reverence to the cry of a bird, the sound of a wave, the words and intentions of a fellow human being. To pay attention means caring enough to honor the needs of ourselves and others in the moment, *caring enough to feel*.

It is a sad and curious testimony to the society in which we live that we pass through life walled up within ourselves, doling out carefully-rationed portions of ourselves at critical moments, to sustain what we feebly call "relationships," while inside we are *dying*. It is my feeling that one of the saddest experiences a human being can have is to exist in the soulless vacuum that relationships in our society have become, unconnected to ourselves or our fellow human beings.

Why exist this way, when we can *live* and open to the possibility of boundless love, peace, joy and health?

The latest statistics show that one in every three Americans will have cancer. To me, this is testimony to the hopelessness, powerlessness and suffering that has become a way of life within dysfunctional families, who in turn must survive within a dysfunctional society that demands impossible standards of physical perfection, while ignoring the authentic inner being.

Is it any wonder people are lost, as I was, seeking a better way?

Cancer is a powerful vehicle for change, because it gets people's attention. Finally, people have to slow down enough to care and feel and recognize who we are. In the finality of the possible imminence of death, we find life.

Cultivating awareness through practices like meditation, relaxation and journaling allows our minds to slow down enough to be able to pay attention and listen to the inner voice and the outer messages we are receiving. In this manner, the intelligence within us is able to chart our pathway towards a sane, healthy, joyous existence.

Our sense of smell is also a powerful receptor. Who could forget the smell of burning leaves, freshly-cut grass or the stars twinkling like crystals in the night sky, a warm spring day, the aroma of roses or fresh-brewed coffee? The scent of a favorite perfume or the smell of the beloved's skin, a newborn baby, fresh lilacs sparkling with dew or white violets in the wood?

One woman I worked with, Barb, said she'd never forget the smell of her grandfather's pipe tobacco. It represented love to her.

Even our sense of taste—lemon on the tongue, a delicious meal, the sweetness of a kiss.

Or touch—silky washed hair, fluffy kittens, the warm body of the beloved, silk or satin, the velvety feel of a butterfly's wing.

Close your eyes and imagine—smelling, tasting and touching these sensations.

The experience of our senses is the experience of life itself.

Seeing Beyond the Surface

> Two men look out through the same bars.
> One sees the mud and one the stars.
>
> —FREDERICK LANGBRIDGE, Cluster of Quiet Thoughts

There is an intelligence within us that sees and knows. As we tap into this intelligence, we are able to see beneath the mundane surface of life and communicate on a higher level.

In actuality, we communicate on two levels. One is the verbal level, the words being expressed; the other is an unspoken, deeper level that allows us to join, heart-to-heart with another, in true communion.

As we become truly feeling human beings with open hearts, as we achieve within ourselves deep health, we gain an ability to see into ourselves and into our fellow human beings in authentic soul connection.

The doors of perception expand, gifts blossom within ourselves, and we are able to see into the hearts of our brothers and sisters, into the hearts of problems to find solutions, and into the heart of life itself to experience peace and bliss.

We are able to believe in what we see. We are able to **know**.

This knowing does not take place in the intellectual mind. Knowing comes from the heart, the inner source. The creative intelligence is a universal unlimited source of answers we can tap into through clarity of mind and heart.

When we believe in ourselves, we develop the capacity to see into the heart of life itself, to pierce through the mystery.

Life becomes a wonderful adventure that we are attuned to with the totality of our being, yet we never know where the rabbit will pop up next! As much as we would like to, we cannot outfox God! Thus life is always a magical, fascinating adventure with new challenges to overcome. Personally, I wouldn't want to live any other way.

Make the conscious choice to open up your eyes so that you may *see*, your ears so that you may *listen*, your *feelings* so that you may *know* reality.

Look into your own eyes so that you may drink deeply when you look into the heart of another, so that you may feel wholeness within and soul communion with your fellow human beings. This is truly being alive.

Exercise:
A. Pick up your pen and begin to write in your journal. Perhaps, like most of us, you will feel a resistance holding you back. Just choose to break through and *do* it! Who knows what you will write? Whatever it is, it will be helpful to you. Before long, you will feel it to be interesting and even *fun*!

B. Pick a spot in nature and close your eyes. Allow your breathing to relax you. What sounds are you aware of? Can you identify the nuances of sound you receive? How does it feel to just sit back and *listen*? Write your awareness in your journal.

C. Sit in a quiet spot and look carefully at a plant, tree or living creature. Observe the quality of light emanating from its source. Look at the aura surrounding the living entity. Many times you may see a white light, or vibrations of light or energy, being released from the organism. If you are observing a human being, be aware of your feelings. Are you able to connect with him or her below the verbal level? Can you feel a bonding or intimacy that is comfortable? Or are you aware of withdrawal and fear in this person? Become sensitive as you slow down in the moment in awareness to receive the non-verbal messages.

Affirmations:

- As I write down my feelings, I feel a release that calms me.

- I am expressing myself.

- My creative power flows through me in comfort and peace.

- I open my ears, listening to the world around me. I am receptive to the guidance I receive by listening.

- I open my eyes as life unveils its holy face to me. I open to the visual guidance I receive.

15

Love is a state in which all problems are resolved.

—J. KRISHNAMURTI

There Is a Way out of Suffering— Service to Mankind

Given the right set of circumstances and unrelenting pressure, through the process of time, a piece of coal transforms into a beautiful diamond.

The process of change within a human being is no different. It seems we grow and change when our backs are up against the wall, and there is no other way. The darkness within ourselves must be enlightened through truth and love. Only then can we sparkle radiantly in our many facets and realize the tremendous value of who we are.

The path of love requires tremendous humility and honesty.

When I first started doing workshops, it took courage to reveal the painful facts of my life and open up to people. I only hoped that somehow my story would help others to grow and change. I knew I needed to share my journey in order to grow myself; yet, I had no idea how this actual telling and sharing over the course of time would result in the healing of my life.

At first, I experienced shame and guilt as I risked being open about my feelings. It was hard to say all the painful things I had to discuss in order to let people in.

However, I began to see that the honesty of my own willingness to share allowed others to open up as well, to unlock the doors within themselves. The total experience was one of *love*.

I began to realize that this is what relationship means: it means *response*. In healing my own relationship with myself, with God's help through love, I was then able to explore honestly with others through the sharing of feelings. As a result, true *intimacy, bonding, and love* resulted.

The more I talked and shared with others, the more I found the negative, shadowy parts of myself become brilliantly alive and illuminated. An acceptance of myself and others was experienced within, and I am now able to know intimately what it means to *love*, and to *feel compassion* and *wholeness*.

Once you realize the beauty of your own inner nature, you are then able to understand that we are all one. The love and compassion you feel within your own self, for your self, then flows forth limitlessly in waves of compassion for your fellow beings, because you realize the divinity existing within the other. This person who crosses your path is not a stranger; he is your brother, and she is your sister.

As your intention or motivation becomes correct, that is, the love of one's self, you are able to balance honoring the needs of others with honoring the needs of yourself. You become a finely-tuned instrument of light, keenly perceptive of your own feelings, and cognizant of the feelings of others. You become an artist of life, mastering the art of living. This is true reverence for life and God, a noble and elegant existence.

Again, I personally wouldn't want to live any other way.

I have finally listened, learned, and healed.

Once a person reaches this level of growth or enlightenment, one does not sit like the statue of Buddha on a shelf and gather dust. New challenges are there to overcome; the universe provides infinite opportunities for us to purify and enlighten our souls, so that we may experience the ecstasy of oneness with the light of God.

When we finally know and realize that loving and serving mankind is the same as loving ourselves, then we are in connection with our purpose in life. We willingly and lovingly assume our responsibility as conscious human beings making conscious choices; we are realizing the reality of our earthly journey; we are learning the lesson we have come to this school on earth to realize. We are honor students who know that *love* is what it is all about! How could we have forgotten?

Mike, a man in my group with pancreatic and liver cancer, was given four months to live. It is now five years later and he has just opened a new business. He even has time to help out at the kitchens serving the homeless.

Mike, the man who healed his inner child, Chuckie, has become a source of strength at AA meetings helping new members get on their path and giving guidance and support to families with cancer.

Marsha, recovering from breast cancer in our support group, has just opened up a service with her partner, Ed, transporting cancer patients from Naples, Florida to the Cleveland Clinic in Fort Lauderdale.

JoAnn helps give support and guidance amnesty sessions to encourage creative expression and unity in her oganization.

Jerri, whose therapist recommended a book on death and dying when she had colon cancer, and who was told she would be on chemotherapy the rest of her life, made a choice for life. Now, after prayer and inner work, she has just returned from a trip to Jerusalem where she journeyed to give thanks for her healing. She is now well.

There are many ways people choose to express gratitude for healing and improve their own health and well-being. Service is the ultimate healing of the ego and the road to further growth and deep health. However, we must always remember to keep a balance within that allows us to love ourselves while helping others.

16

God helps those who persevere.

—Koran

All justice comes from God. He alone is its source.

—Jean Jacques Rousseau

He who loses his life shall find it.

—Jesus

Further Miracles:
I Reacquire the Custody
of My Children

In turning to God in my need, taking on the responsibility of my life and health, and believing that one day a purpose and path would be revealed to me, I was able to let go of the past and create a new life as an authentically powered human being.

I had to keep believing in a better way.

God revealed the way to me. The path to that way is as unique as every human being; yet the way is the same for all of us.

During the years of separation from my children as the custodial parent, we kept in touch by phone almost every day; after my practice, Self-Healing, really took off, I was able to fly them down to be with me for the summer and Christmas holidays. During the intervals, I would fly up to Canada, to be with them. Our bonding and intimacy was maintained, nurtured; our love for each other grew and flourished.

It became evident that their father's patterns of abuse had surfaced and were now activated upon my children. Legally, I was tied up in knots and everything I tried to do to unravel the knot ended in frustration and despair.

I had to live with and accept the situation as it was. My dear friend Bernie Siegel advised me to call Silent Unity and ask them to pray about the situation; this I did many times. It always helped.

As time went on, the neglect and abuse of my children continued until it reached a point where the children literally begged me to help them out of the situation.

I looked within myself and struggled to find the will of God. Through grave introspection, prayer and meditation, I determined that it was God's will that I go forward to help my children. Even though the situation still remained hopeless legally, I knew that if it was God's will that I take action, I would succeed. This did not prevent me from shaking in my boots as I put my life on the line once again to take a major risk.

Financially, there was no way I could afford to do this. Travel expenses and legal bills would be phenomenal even for the wealthy, and I was not in that category. I prayed and then began to take action. Soon, events began to shape themselves in a recognizable pattern to assist me. I began to realize that my intuition was correct; God's will was at work in the situation.

First, my ex-husband's parents visited with me and offered their support. They encouraged me to make an application for custody. This was a shocking turn of events, and a tremendous healing for me, personally.

Then one of my dear clients talked to a billionaire who owned a winter residence in Naples about the plight of my children. This man gave her the name of a top attorney in Canada, and the number to call.

The attorney's name is Peter Mockler and my first conversation with him convinced me that the entire chain of events had the blessing of God.

You have to realize the total impossibility of the situation. When I related my story to Peter, he responded, "I'll get your children back for you."

When I relayed my doubts to him regarding the legal system, he replied, "They just don't know who you are yet. The situation hasn't been explained to them properly. You just have to be like Winston Churchill and *never give up.*"

When I heard these words spoken to me, a chill ran up my spine. I then KNEW. These were the very same words spoken by myself in my lectures and to my clients about perseverance: "You just have to remember the words of Winston Churchill, when asked the secret of his great success: Never, never, never, never, never give up!" How often had I spoken these words!

This was a tremendous affirmation for me. Once again, God was winking his eye at me saying, "Do not fear. I am with you."

When I sent my first correspondence to Peter, I found his address to be none other than Churchill Row!

This was just the start of one of the hardest things I have ever done. It was a tremendous leap of faith for me. I had to overcome every buried fear and guilt imaginable within myself to keep going forward and believe my path was lit for myself and my children.

I advised my children to stand up for themselves and speak their truth. I told them they had the power to change their lives, that truth, love and courage would break down all the doors and set us free.

The children took a tremendous risk. In speaking up for themselves, they were taken out of their father's home and placed in foster care. Through God's grace they were all placed together in the care of a family in a small country town. They had to live there for three months until the date of the trial.

The trial is a book in itself. Five attorneys were present—an attorney for the Province, my ex-husband's counsel, Peter Mockler and Mia Devoe representing myself, and a private attorney representing the children.

It was a supreme battle and test of endurance for four days and four nights. My dear friend and secretary Carol Jean Brooks came up with me and sat by my side, and thank God she did; it was a grueling trial. My ex-husband's father testified on my and the children's behalf. Peter and Mia had their hearts involved in the outcome and we buoyed up each others' spirits and battled it all the way.

Speaking up for ourselves in court was an ultimate healing for me and the children. Finally, the truth was spoken. The verdict was given after midnight on the fourth evening. It was a triumph of faith. I was given custody of my beloved boys.

It was a tremendous lesson for all of us. Most of all, we now know and realize that we have the power to change our destinies, that each day is too sacred to waste, that **Love** conquers all, and to *never, never, never, never, never give up!*

Affirmations:

These loving affirmations are helpful to realize the state of mind that heals all wounds and resolves all suffering.

- God's love is flowing through me, giving me the courage to act and speak my truth.

- There is nothing to fear. I am SAFE.

- God is speaking through me.

- The words I say are right and appropriate.

- God is acting through me.

- My actions are in accord with God's will.

- My life is divinely guided and protected.

- I feel the strength of God's love as a power and an energy.

- I now go forth with courage to claim my good.

- As I love and support myself, so does God and the universe support me.

- God's will is my will.

- ❧ I am on my path in life.
- ❧ All the help I need is here for me.
- ❧ I am safe.
- ❧ I am opening to receive the gifts of love that are here for me.
- ❧ I am opening to receive God.
- ❧ I am worthy to receive the grace of God.
- ❧ I am grateful for my many blessings.
- ❧ I am grateful to God, to myself, and to the wonderful people who give me unconditional love and support.
- ❧ I now receive this love with gratitude and joy.

17

I Have a Dream

A dream or vision has great power. A vision, if it is strong enough in the mind, has the power to heal a body. A dream that is born of passionate feeling in the heart of a human being comes from the very source of creation, and has the power to heal a life. If it is strong enough, it becomes a force that can heal the world.

Healing starts within each one of us, spreads to our relationships, to the family and community, and then to the planet. Each one of us commands a force within that is able to cause a revolution of consciousness that can change our inner world from war to peace. When each one of us knows and believes that *we are the world*, then we have become conscious, responsible human beings, capable of greatness and genius, capable of love. We are free.

I believe that we are at a crossroads in human life as we know it. There are forces at work in the world today attempting to heal the planet and illuminate the human beings who hold the answers to the future of our species.

A wish, a dream, a hope, a prayer: these are the invisible tools with which we create our future. A belief has the power to heal, if the faith exists to support it.

I had the courage to lift myself up from the ashes with the help of God, and start to believe in myself. Someone once said to me that it takes only one person to believe in you and for me that person was Bernie Siegel.

I guess God must have connected us, because in Bernie I was able to see and feel the genius and compassion I could respect and respond to. I saw that his work grew out of a true love and reverence for people, that he is a true humanitarian. One day I saw Bernie on a talk show trying to explain his philosophy of healing to a group of doctors who were battling fiercely to discredit him. This was in the early days, when Bernie had his work cut out for him.

"You see," he was saying, regarding his patients, "I love them, and then they start to get well." The look on his face when he said these words was one of true compassion and humility. I will never forget how he looked when he said that. I thought to myself, "Aha! That is the key! To love them, and then they heal." How simple. Thank you, Bernie. I love you.

Since then, I have been loving people in my practice, Self-Healing, in my family, my children and my life. I love the people who cross my path in life, even if they are exceedingly unlovable; I can't help it, I love them anyway. I even love the little lizards that hop and leap in the bushes near my home, the birds flying cheerfully about their business in the palm trees, and the exquisite raindrops falling just for me as I write these words on this cool, beautiful evening.

My children are with me now; we are all growing and healing. In the process of change that is called life, love is the glue that holds it all together, unconditional love and acceptance. It is a joy for me to provide a climate of love for my children and to watch them respond and grow.

The many clients and families who have come through my door at Self-Healing have become more than that; they are loving friends and family. I continue to see a purpose to it all as they grow and change the world around them with their love and intelligence.

They, as I, needed permission to live, to enjoy, to feel, to love, to be. If you need that permission yourself, please allow it. I know the world could use it.

How inspiring and moving it is to me to see the divine thread that has run through my life, illuminating the mystery. I see so clearly the divine plan, the divine intelligence at work in all things, in all creation. It is all so simple, if we let it be.

One day, years ago, I picked up a book called *Love, Medicine and Miracles* at a point of crisis in my life. That book, the author of that book, and the author of the author of that book, started the healing process of my life.

Since then, how things have changed! What a difference a day can make.

That difference can be a miracle.

If one of you reads these words and feels the value of them, I hope you use them as seeds of love to start a beautiful garden within yourself. I wish for you that the fruits and flowers of that garden flow forth from you in health and abundance, and that you are able to expand in consciousness and experience the divinity within. That is my wish for you all. This book is sent with love from me to you. Godspeed.

Appendices

The Path of Life Chart

I have found this Path of Life Chart to be the human journey of the soul from birth into adulthood—the inner and outer life experiences and human dynamics that give birth to dysfunctional patterns, and then the recovery process, which leads into healing, authenticity and health.

This chart represents the understanding of human experience I have gleaned from my own inner journey and my work with others at Self-Healing. If you study it closely, looking inside yourself for parallels and realization, you will find it quite astonishing and revolutionary in its information and impact.

It can be used for guidance and direction.

If you study this outline, you will be able to pinpoint your life's journey, the birth of destructive patterns, and guidance for the healing process of recovery.

For example, you will notice that, according to the Path of Life Chart, many people turn away from love to the control mode after being hurt or rejected in first love.

This choice in itself is a decision not to *feel*, and it causes a human being to become intellectualized. That choice in itself results in a shift in values and priorities that is destructive and superficial. Over the passage of time, *just this in itself* causes a hardening of the human being and a loss of connection to the soul.

One man I worked with in recovery for alcoholism and cancer shook with sobs as he realized that he had closed his heart forty years earlier after losing his first love. He was totally astonished and amazed as he allowed the pain of the experience to surface for the first time. I cried with him through this painful realization. Since then he has worked at opening his heart to tenderness and vulnerability. His is opening to love.

This is one aspect of the chart.

Use the wisdom and information here to work on yourself. Write your feelings and discoveries in your journal. You will find this chart in itself quite amazing and helpful, if you take the time to process it and study it carefully.

Form a loving group and share realizations and experiences. You will find your inner world changing as your understanding of your "Path of Life" is illuminated.

Journey forward in the process toward your soul's recovery—your authentic being and deep health.

May the grace of God be with you.

Path of Life: Journey of Self From Birth—Dysfunctional Patterns —Recovery Process—Health—Authentic Self

As infants, we are totally feeling in our response. The intellect is not sufficiently developed to deter us from authenticity and intuition. The creative source flows freely without obstruction.

INFANCY —Total feeling and response
- No intellect or ego
- Total intuition
- Oneness
- Wonder
- Awe

Although our children today are becoming intellectualized at an early age, the ego is not yet in control. Children, because of their lack of ego, are able to experience the flexibility and spontaneity necessary to be present within the moment.

The following list incorporates essentially the "heaven within" of childhood.

CHILDHOOD—Lack of Ego
- Reliance on inner source (creative intelligence)
- Trust and reliance on perception
- Total acceptance
- Trust
- Joy
- Love
- Peace
- Acceptance of feelings
- Courage
- Passion for life
- Wonder
- Awe
- Magic
- Wholeness

The intellectual mind gains control through Conditioning. Life comes in with painful experience. The sensitive intelligence within the child becomes submerged by fear, anger, shame and guilt. The intellect begins to take precedence over the feeling self.

CONDITIONING—Parents
- Schools, Teachers
- Education
- Demands to behave in certain manner for acceptance
- Behavior for approval
- Abuse
- Criticism
- Control
- Abandonment by one or both parents (death, divorce, emotional withdrawal)
- Experience of injustice
- Experience of betrayal

The painful experience of rejection or loss in first love causes a suppression of feelings. There is an unconscious decision to turn away from love, to be *in control*. By this time there is a loss of trust, a submergence of the true self. The intellect is in command, therefore cherished dreams of love and happiness are often put aside. Money, acquisition of material objects, power and external stimulation all become priorities. The pain/pleasure syndrome triggers addiction. All of the above results in a loss of trust in self, God and the universe. The human being is in *fear of change*.

FIRST LOVE—Rejection
• Hurt
• Abandonment
• Suppression of feelings—remains denied and unhealed

HUMAN RESPONSE—Decision to turn away from Love
• Decision to be in control
• Denial of feelings
• Denial of truth
• Negative beliefs about self
• Being in control—living life according to intellect, and what you "should" do, instead of realizing cherished dreams of what you want to do.
• Loss of trust in self and God
• Loss of intensity

RESULTS—Fear of Change
• Obstruction of soul's flow or creative source

Destructive patterns emerge with loss of trust and lack of connection to feelings and God. The human being is now in denial. Full-blown addictions are manifested.

The human being wears either a mask of convention and morality, participating in a secret life or secret fantasy world, or is in open rebellion.

RESULTANT DESTRUCTIVE LIFE PATTERNS — Being mired in dead relationships, in stagnant, molded, conditioned life.
- Living life according to what you "should" do for the approval of others, society
- Denial of Feelings
- Hypocrisy
- Secrecy
- Secret fantasy inner world
- Work addiction to avoid intimacy and emotional responsibility
- Alcoholism
- Drug abuse
- Food addiction
- Sexual addiction
- Criminal behavior

OR—Hedonistic rebellion vs. authority
- Sexual promiscuity
- Avoidance of intimacy
- Alcoholism
- Drug abuse
- Criminal behavior
- Sexual addiction

Life is now lived based on fear. Life in the fear mode is exhausting and demanding as the individual can never be Perfect and, as a result, is *never good enough.*

The focus is on material gain and approval of society. The intellect is merciless in its stresses, criticisms and demands. Over the passage of time, the true human being is lost.

Living in this manner is a destructive course. The stresses take their toll. Life itself intervenes in crisis.

LIVING LIFE BASED ON FEAR
- Need to be PERFECT
- Denial of feelings, feeling self.

- Lack of connection to self, God.
- Lack of joy
- Focus on striving for material objects, success.
- Lack of simplicity
- Enslavement to "inner drivers"
- Hidden feelings of worthlessness
- Fear of failure
- Fear of LOVE
- ANGER (at self and others)
- GUILT (for abandoning self, sexuality, NOT BEING GOOD ENOUGH)
- Resentment
- STRESS (straining to uphold an image of who you are not)
- Strong inner critic—judgmental, cynical
- Blaming others—refusal to TAKE RESPONSIBILITY

PASSAGE OF TIME—False Values
- Lack of priorities in values
- Approval seeking behavior
- Living in the ego
- Loss of connection with feelings
- Separation of mind and body
- Inability to relax
- Lack of spiritual awareness

LIVING LIFE IN FEAR OF CHANGE
CRISIS—Serious Illness
- Alcoholism
- Drug addiction
- Sexual addiction
- Financial crisis
- Hopelessness
- Infidelity
- Marital crisis
- Divorce

- Falling in love
- Abandonment
- Break-up of family
- Death of a loved one

The time has come to face up to yourself, to the facts of your life, and take charge or die. The old life, the old self, must fall away and a new life, a new self, emerge. Spiritual transformation is in effect. A choice must be made and responsibility assumed.

RECOVERY PROCESS —Awareness of human mortality
- Shattering of illusion
- Focus shifts from need for approval from others to need to know and love self
- Reaching out for help
- Honesty
- Stepping out of Fear to Risk BEING WHO YOU ARE
- Revolution of spirit
- Loving and supporting the self
- Release of pain in expression of feelings
- Questioning all authority, conditioning by parents, schools, relationships, society
- Ending or renewal of relationships, career, finances
- Burning desire to know truth, love, what life is all about
- Burning desire to know how to live
- Finding out what you believe
- Finding the truth through love, passion to know
- Courage to change, take risks
- Release of guilt, anger, resentment, fear through inner work and understanding of self
- Learning to love and accept yourself
- Unconditional love
- Unending hope through unbearable struggle, sorrow, refusal to give up
- Perseverance through all odds
- Openness—end of secrets, hiding

In the recovery process, we search for truth. The first awareness is that we are not in control of life. The ego and perhaps even the human being faces the reality of the possibility of death. The denial system cracks.

This awareness triggers a process of change within the human being.

Perfect honesty is essential in uncovering your true feelings in regard to yourself, your family, your relationships, your life. Choices are made, courageous actions are taken on the basis of beliefs and priorities.

The focus shifts from the material to the spiritual. Feelings are brought forth and shared honestly. There is a shift in priorities and values. The need for love and connection is essential. The soul is in recovery. The human being searches to find the true path, the true meaning of life. The will to live is kindled. There is a willingness to feel emotional vulnerability, tenderness. The deeper questions and needs demand to be addressed.

There is a need for answers and the humble awareness that these answers can only be found by asking. The human being turns to God for help through prayer. There is a spiritual awakening.

The human being takes responsibility for his/her life. The illusion, the denial system, is cracked through *feeling* experience. The human being seeks connection to God.

Inner work is a necessity to find and uproot negative beliefs and emotional blocks. Inner healing causes joy and happiness and a return to feelings.

Love is a priority. The soul's flow is unblocked as unconditional love takes the place of fear.

The creative process is stimulated by meditation, visualization and emotional honesty.

The human being finds the true path in life. As a result, a feeling of love, protection and connection cause joy, wonder and awe.

Life becomes a mystical experience. There is a magical sequence of "coincidences" that happen to support the individual in the quest for authenticity.

The kundalini energy rises, bringing renewal of the life force. The division between heart and mind is healed. Wholeness is experienced.

A sense of oneness and compassion accompanies personal freedom and unconditional love. There is awareness of the presence of God. Inner peace is found.

SPIRITUAL AWAKENING
- Prayer
- Meditation
- Letting go to God
- TAKING RESPONSIBILITY
- Humbleness, Gratitude
- Humility
- Grace, living in the light
- Spiritual awareness
- Forgiveness
- Connection to inner voice
- Acceptance of change as part of life
- Belief in self, perceptions, inner truth
- Courage
- Risk
- LOVE
- Healing the inner child
- Letting go of past through inner healing
- Renewal of trust
- Return to right values, right speech, right behavior, right action, right relationship
- Attention in the HERE AND NOW
- Spiritual renewal of connection with nature
- View of earth and its creatures as sacred
- Switch from intellect to wisdom of the body, heart, creative intelligence

- Return to SIMPLICITY
- Return of intensity of feeling, expression of feelings, courage to feel
- Serendipity
- Affirmations of God as answer to prayer
- Wonder
- Awe
- Passion for Life
- Compassion
- Unblocking of creative life force, sexuality, kundalini energy
- Emergence of a new human being, your own authority
- Personal freedom, joy
- Wholeness
- Oneness
- Wellness
- Inner peace
- Total renewal

HEALTH ****************************** HEALTH

Affirmations

These loving affirmations are helpful to realize the state of mind that heals all wounds and resolves all suffering.

- I am healthy and strong and free of all illness.
- I love and accept myself exactly as I am, and I am taking care of me.
- As I love and support myself, so does God and the universe support me.
- Golden opportunities are everywhere for me.
- My courageous stand for health is calming my emotions and healing my body.
- I love and accept myself as I am.
- I accept all my feelings, even the negative ones.
- In this acceptance I pass through the negative into the positive.
- In this acceptance there is love.
- The love heals me and allows me to grow.
- I accept other people as they are with all their imperfections.
- In this acceptance my Iron Will of Ignorance relaxes, and I accept the Will of God.
- I emerge from this painful demanding ego into the light of God where there is humility, acceptance, love and peace.
- Acceptance is the key for me today.
- I am good enough.

- I lovingly enfold the child that is myself with the white light of unconditional love.

- I am opening to receive the gifts of love that are here for me.

- I am opening to receive God.

- I am worthy to receive the grace of God.

- I let go of the misery of the past.

- I let go of my belief that life cannot be wonderful and joyful.

- I realize this is a false belief based on painful experience of childhood.

- I open to the belief that life is wonderful and good and I am ready and open to receive my good.

- I am grateful for my many blessings.

- I am grateful to the wonderful helpers on my path who gave me and continue to give me unconditional love.

- I now receive this love with gratitude and joy.

- I am free to live a joyful life.

- I am free to be who I am.

- I allow the joy and innocence of the natural world to flow through my being, healing me.

- I feel the mystery and enchantment of the nature spirits, my animal friends, as a source of inner peace and wonder.

- I give thanks to the Earth, my mother and friend.

- My connection with the plants, insects and animals of this beautiful world fortifies my soul and gives me hope.

- I see and feel the presence of God in all living things.

- I feel the hum and throb of the earth's heartbeat as a cosmic healing energy.

- This reverence makes me whole and free.

- I am one with the divine Creator. I am free.

- It is safe for me to remember my dreams.

- It is safe for me to explore within myself.

- I open myself to receive the wisdom of the Universe for use as guidance and direction in my life.

- All is well in my world.

- God's love is flowing through me, giving me the courage to act and speak my truth.

- There is nothing to fear. I am safe.

- God is speaking through me.

- The words I say are right and appropriate.

- God is acting through me.

- My actions are in accord with God's will.

- My life is divinely guided and protected.

- I feel the strength of God's love as a power and an energy.

- I now go forth with courage to claim my good.

- God's will is my will.

- I am on my path in life.

- All the help I need is here for me.

- I am safe.

- As I write down my feelings, I feel a release that calms me.

- I am expressing myself.

- My creative power flows through me in comfort and peace.

- I open my ears, listening to the world around. I am receptive to the guidance I receive by listening.

- I open my eyes as life unveils its holy face to me. I open to the visual guidance I receive.

- God's love is flowing through me, giving me the courage to act and speak my truth.

Meditations

Prepare a special place for yourself in your home, perhaps a special chair, a sacred picture, a candle. Though you can meditate anywhere, at anytime, simply by closing your eyes, it is a comforting feeling to know that you have a place to go that is yours alone to be at peace and go within the silence of yourself. This is your holy space.

Perhaps you can also keep your journal there to record feelings and inner reflection. You are worth this attention.

Each meditation will lead you inward through different areas and aspects of yourself. Each time you sit back, closing your eyes to meditate, you are experiencing yourself. You are refreshing yourself. Be aware of renewed vitality.

When thoughts intrude, simply, very gently and lovingly, bring your attention back to your meditation.

Perhaps you will want to record these meditations in your own voice to play back to yourself. Or, these same meditations are available on tape to you by writing to the address in this book.

Relax and enjoy your inner journey. Don't forget to write in your journal!

Record what you experienced during your meditation. Write it down in your journal. What were your feelings and reflections? What are you learning about yourself on your inner journey?

Inner Child Meditation

Feel your body relaxing. . . . Allow a very peaceful feeling, starting at the top of your head, and allow all the muscles in your scalp, to relax. . . .

And feel your mind relaxing. . . . Allow any thoughts to drift, and fade away. . . . As a sense of peace and serenity flows through your mind, feel your mind relaxing . . . as you begin to focus your attention, on the number 7. . . .

Visualize, in your mind's eye, a black velvet curtain. . . . Against this black velvet curtain you see emblazoned, in bright gold, the number 7. . . . You watch as the number 7 becomes vibrant and shining . . . and then begins, slowly, to dissolve and disappear . . . and, in its place, appears a bright, golden number 6. . . .

Imagine the gold number 6, shining against the black velvet curtain, becoming brighter . . . and brighter . . . until it disappears . . . and in its place is a bright . . . golden . . . vibrant . . . number 5. . . .

Watch as the number 5 blazes brightly against the black curtain . . . until, finally, it too begins to dissolve . . . and disappear. . . . In its place is a bright golden number 4. . . .

Visualize the golden number 4 . . . shining . . . burning brightly against the black velvet curtain, until it, too, begins to dissolve and disappear . . . and in its place is a beautiful vibrant number 3. . . .

Visualize the beautiful, golden number 3, shining brightly, and then dissolving . . . and disappearing . . . and, in its place, a bright golden number 2 appears. . . .

See the beautiful, shining, golden number 2, so vividly outlined against the black velvet curtain, burning brightly . . . until it, too, begins to dissolve and disappear . . . and in its place appears a golden number 1. . . .

Watch as the number 1 turns more and more golden . . . brighter and brighter . . . until it slowly dissolves . . . and disappears . . . and you feel yourself relaxing . . . a beautiful sense of

peace and relaxation permeates your mind and your body. . . .
Feel yourself drifting, without fear, towards a beautiful place of
peace inside yourself, knowing that there is nothing to fear . . .
that you are safe . . . and you visualize, in your mind's eye, a
beautiful white rosebud . . . and this beautiful, pure, white
rosebud is your heart center. . . .

As you concentrate on your breath, and concentrate on
breathing in only peace and love . . . you watch as the velvety
petals of the rose begin to unfold. . . . With every breath of peace
and love that you take . . . the beautiful, velvety petals of the
white rose unfold before your eyes. . . .

As the rose opens, you see a little child . . . and you are so
amazed and joyful to realize that this little child is you . . . and
this little child holds out its arms to you, and you go up to the
little child, and you hold your little child . . . and stroke your
little child's hair, and make your little child feel very, very
peaceful . . . and very loved . . . and very, very safe. . . .

And you look into the eyes of your little child, and you say,
*I love and accept you exactly as you are. . . . There is nothing to
fear. . . . You are safe. . . . I am here for you. . . . I will take care
of you, and protect you. . . .*

And you make your little child feel very loved, and very
safe . . . and you play with your little child. . . . You are so happy
to be together again . . . and it feels so good to be together, to
be loving each other. . . .

You find yourself enjoying your little child, and you play
together, in innocence . . . in laughter . . . and joy . . . feeling
the love and peace that you may have never known before. . . .

And now you see that your little child has something in its
hand for you . . . and, as your little child opens its hand, your
little child gives to you a beautiful crystal; as you touch your
little child's fingers reaching to take the crystal, a magnificent,
white light flows through the crystal into both of your hands . . .
filling both you and your little child with a beautiful spiritual
radiance . . . and you know that something very extraordinary,
something very special is happening. . . . You watch as the

beautiful colors are emitted from the crystal, beautiful colors of purple . . . and silver . . . oranges . . . and blue . . . red and green . . . and you realize that your little child is giving to you the power . . . the energy . . . the faith . . . the love . . . and the trust in life that is the power of the little child to live in the present moment, as the only moment that truly exists. . . .

And you allow yourself to be filled with the power of your little child. . . . Feel the power and energy flow through you . . . and accept with humbleness and gratitude this gift of your inner child. . . . Know that all your inner child asks in return is that your little child feel very, very safe . . . and secure . . . and that you take care of this little child, knowing that your little child is important . . . that this child is sacred . . . and must be honored . . . and that in honoring this little child, the child will give to you power and belief . . . so that you may instill this power in your life, for inner peace and healing. . . .

Now you thank your little child for this beautiful gift which you cherish . . . and you hug, and you love, this little child . . . and you say again, *I love and accept you exactly as you are. . . . You are so beautiful . . . you are worthy . . . you are good enough just the way you are. . . .*

You nestle your little child, snuggling within the heart of the rose once again, knowing that your child is there for you . . . that you are there for each other in love . . . unconditional love and peace . . . for the being that is you. . . .

You are filled with a deep serenity as you watch without fear . . . in trust . . . as the petals of the rose enclose your little child once again. . . .

You thank your little child for the beautiful gift and you feel the power of the gift inside you . . . as an energy and a force and a power that you can use in your life today . . . to make choices that are healthy for you . . . choices that can assist you in your inner healing . . . in your inner growth . . . choices based on trust, and peace and faith . . . choices made on behalf of the being that is you . . . choices made in support of the love that you hold for yourself. . . .

You feel a deep sense of calm, a deep sense of well being, knowing that your life is always divinely protected and guided and that there is truly nothing to fear . . . that you are safe and that a life lived in belief and in support of the love in one's self is a powerful life. . . . Bless yourself for taking this time for you. . . . You deserve it. . . . You are honoring yourself. . . . You are loved and I love you. . . . Feel yourself returning once again, without fear, into consciousness with a deep sense of well being and inner peace that you will carry into your day . . . honoring the present moment as being the only moment that truly exists . . . honoring yourself with all the choices that you make, and knowing that *as you love and support yourself, so does God and the universe support you*. . . . When you feel comfortable, open your eyes. You are worthy, you are honored, you are *loved*. . . .

Butterfly Meditation

Feel yourself relaxing. . . . Close your eyes. . . .

Take a *deep breath*, then let it out. . . . Feel a wave of relaxation rippling through you, starting from the top of your head and flowing through all your internal organs, through every cell of your body, relaxing you. . . .

Feel yourself slipping deeply within, knowing that there is nothing to fear, that you are safe. Feel the beauty and comfort of a deep source of love and peace within yourself.

Visualize a beautiful scene in nature, a spot where you feel very peaceful and relaxed. Breathe in the purity of the air, the green of the vegetation, the sparkling clarity of the healing waters. . . .

Imagine that you are a colorful caterpillar crawling upon a leafy branch. Feel yourself attach firmly to a spot on the branch as a change takes place in your consciousness. You are surrounded and enveloped in a gauzy shell. Feel the silence within your haven, the stillness and protection you are experiencing. . . . Allow a sense of comfort and acceptance to be received within yourself. . . . You are changing. Slip deeply within the acceptance of that change. . . .

Now feel within yourself the need to emerge and expand. Visualize yourself poking a hole through your gauzy cocoon. . . . Effortlessly, squeeze through the hole out into the open air. . . .

Feel the wonder and freedom of your escape! Take a look at the wonder and beauty in the world. . . . You are NEW, a magical Being. Experience the unfoldment of your new self. There is a source of power uplifting you. Up, up you float on the currents of air, your glorious wings empowering your flight. . . . Experience the beauty of who you are. Feel the freedom and delight of your freedom. It is fun to be you!

Beneath you, view the beauty of the earth. Visualize the gorgeous, colorful flowers, the emerald green trees and plants, the silent beauty of the animals and insects. Feel your oneness with all living things. You are the Butterfly, the animal, the tree, the insect. You are in silent unity with all life, all creation. Fly and soar with the birds, the dragonflies, the clouds. . . .

Feel the beauty of your freedom. You are awake, alive. You are FREE.

Allow yourself to experience a sense of total peace and love.

As you return to consciousness, bless yourself for having the courage to be who you are. . . . Allow the love and respect you feel for yourself to overflow onto all others who cross your path this day. Do not be afraid to be sensitive, alive. Awaken to the beauty and mystery of life and nature; awaken to who you are. . . .

Hammock of Light

Take a deep breath and let it out. Feel yourself expelling negative energies.

Close your eyes; feel yourself relaxing. Feel a deep source of peace within yourself. Slip gently inside, without fear. Love and peace—this is who you are.

Now visualize yourself resting in a beautiful hammock made of light. This radiant hammock is composed of illuminated fibers of light, and it is suspended from the points of stars. . . . Beneath the hammock, you can see the outstretched hands of God, illuminated in brilliant white light; the hands are ever-present, always protecting and guiding you, ready to catch you should you fall.

Feel the total peace within yourself, the divine order and harmony of the Universe, the beauty of the night sky. Breathe in the love and peace of the Universe. All the help you need is there for you. Rest in the warm comfort of this truth. . . .

Look before you—your path is lit with stars, sparkling and twinkling like the Milky Way. This is your path in life. Be at peace. It is lit for you. All you need to do is slow down, and walk it with faith and love. . . .

Do not be afraid to feel the excitement of it all, the wonder of the mystery. You are an adventure, just waiting to be explored!

Feel the presence of the light. . . . Allow it to guide and protect you. Remember that light, that love, is who you are.

Allow yourself to return now to the love. Experience the oneness, the total peace. Remember who you are.

Now, feel yourself again awakening into consciousness. You are bringing with you the memory of rest in the hammock of light. Within you is a joy and peace you may have never felt before. Bring this peace into your actions, your choices, your relationships on this blessed day. Enjoy your experience.

How the Woolly Bear Got His Coat

An Allegory of Spiritual Transformation

When I lived in my log cabin in the woods, bedtime was a special time for myself and the children. I would spin endless stories and yarns for their entertainment, education and enjoyment. I didn't realize it then, but these stories were emerging from the source of creation and had great significance.

When I moved down to Florida, before founding Self-Healing, I began writing down some of the stories I had told the children, in order to preserve them. As a child, I dreamed of becoming a writer and have always used poetry and the written word as a means of releasing my feelings through creative expression.

In the fall, the children would collect little woolly bear caterpillars from the fields and put a few in a jar in their room. It was fascinating to watch the darling little woolly bears spin their cocoons. There they would lie dormant until the spring. One spring day, my children and I had the great privilege of observing a miracle. We gazed, fascinated, as the little creatures worked their way out of their cocoons in full butterfly regalia.

Speechless with wonder, we watched as the newly-transformed woolly bears flew about the bedroom and then out the window.

This story is the result of that remarkable experience. I didn't know it then, but it was more than just a fairy tale. It was the story of my life.

Try this idea yourself. Write a fairy tale and then read what you have created. What personal significance lies in what you have written? Reflect upon your ideas.

HOW THE WOOLLY BEAR GOT HIS COAT

Now, children, you remember back to when Woolly Bears were only skinny little hairless things, sort of like black worms that shivered in the grass, don't you? You don't? Well, that was a long, long time ago, a time between ages, when creatures were first developing on this earth, a time very few people remember. It's possible that I'm about the only one left who does remember, so that's why I'm going to write it all down, so that you can know the story too. It was told to me directly by a woolly bear, an old timer wearing one of the original coats. I found him at the top of a dried-up stalk of wild grass, taking in the autumn sun, and this is the story he was good enough to tell me. It's a true one, too. So, listen, or you might miss something.

Once upon a time, in a far off place, there lived a woolly bear. Now, at that time, so long ago, they weren't called woolly bears. Oh, no. They weren't furry and cozy-looking yet. They were black and kind of skinny, and shiny as snakes. In fact, back then, they were called "slimy strings." It wasn't a very nice-sounding name, but then, they weren't very pretty-looking creatures, either. So, you can't really blame anyone for calling them slimy strings.

Now, at that time, slimy strings didn't live through the winter either. They were so skinny, hairless and, well, so down-right slimy that they all kind of died off in winter, and then somehow started up again in the spring; no one knows just how. Even the old-timer didn't know the answer to that, and if anyone would, it was him.

So, anyway, in this long ago time, in a field of tall grass and purple clover, there lived a slimy string named, well, named Slimy.

Slimy was a poetic creature who loved to inch his way to the top of the tallest timothy in the field and stand up on his back pairs of legs, stretching up as high as he could toward the shining sun, while the grass stalk he was perched on got to swaying in the summer breezes.

There he would sit, as kingly a slimy string as anyone would ever find, staring in rapturous wonder at the towering spruces and maples, and at the gorgeous, colorful flowers that dotted the woods and fields. Slimy was in heaven. He had no family and very few close friends, but that didn't stop Slimy from feeling, well, feeling downright happy most of the time. For, you see, Slimy had a good and pure heart, and he saw beauty and goodness in most living things and was happy inside himself.

Sometimes he would make up poems and songs and recite them out loud to the friendly, whistling wind.

"Oh! (breathed he)—
I'm as happy as a string could be.
With the wondrous earth and flowers
As my song,
How could I ever go wrong—"

And the whistling wind would whistle along with him, and the merry sun shine a little brighter in the sky.

Slimy was so filled with childlike delight at just simple everyday things that he wanted it to never end. Every new day was different and exciting to Slimy; he didn't get in a rut too often like other slimy strings. He knew there just wasn't enough time to spend without a smile, when the world was filled with so many beautiful, interesting things, and he was one of them!

So, as time went on, other strings found Slimy a fun creature to be around, and they went out of their way to visit his grass stalk during the day and have long talks with him. In this relaxed and flowing manner, Slimy made some very nice friends.

The summer passed, sunny and eventful; the colorful flowers bloomed and died, and the sweet wild berries were eaten in the wood. Soon, the shiny green leaves of summer were turning crisp and golden, and a hint of Jack Frost filled the once balmy air.

Slimy and his friends shivered at night on their swaying grass stalks. They lived for morning, when the sun would rise high in the sky, warming the chill from their skinny little bodies and bringing them heat and comfort once again.

One fall morning, Slimy looked all around him from his vantage point at the top of the stalk. The leaves on the birch, ash, and maple were turning blazing red and gold; they looked amazing against the always green spruces and pines. In the fields, the goldenrod grew tall and spiky amidst the snowy white everlastings in the silver and gold autumn grasses. The air was clear and sparkling, with an unusual quality of light that shimmered exquisitely on all living things.

Slimy's pure little heart was filled to bursting as a song burst forth from his lips:

"O World,
Splendid are you,
With mysterious ways.
Forever, forever
I will sing for you,
All the rest of my days!"

"Well!" huffed a pair of geese, who had landed nearby in the weeds. "All the rest of your days, indeed!"

One of the geese waddled over and peered closely at Slimy. "Fact is, your days are numbered."

Slimy drew back in shock. "How do you mean, numbered?"

The goose, whose name was Mother, drew herself up, puffing her feathers for warmth. "Can't you feel the chill in the air? You're a string, aren't you? You strings will all be gone by the time the first snow flies."

"Gone?" said Slimy. "Gone where?"

"Dead," said the other goose, whose name was Father. "Strings only live for the season. Look at your friends, shivering and shaking. Why, look at yourself. You're not made to stand the winter. We're not made to stand it either, as far as that goes."

Father stretched his wings. "That's why God gave us wings to fly with. We're on our way south right now. Go there every year. We have to—or we'd be dead, too."

Slimy's eyes widened to full capacity. "Dead! It's not possible. I'm too happy to die! That will never happen to me!"

The two geese looked back and forth at each other. "You mean, you didn't know?"

"Know?" said Slimy. "Well, of course, I had heard things, rumors to be sure, but. . . ."

"Afraid it's true, old chap," said a gruff voice nearby.

Slimy looked over to see a tall string swinging from a stalk of goldenrod.

"Hi!" said the tall string. "My name's Noodle. I heard about it from one of the older strings. Jack will be here soon, blowing his frosty breath our way. That'll be the last of us strings, I'm afraid."

"No!" protested Slimy. "It just CAN'T be. Why, I love these trees and flowers, these friendly fields, too much to ever say good-bye!" And he began to weep softly.

The two geese looked at one another. "You and your big mouth," said Father to Mother.

Mother, sorry now, asked quietly, "Would you like to hop a ride with us? We"re flying to sunny lands. Chances are you'd be all right there."

"And leave my home, my friends, my wind and sun and starry skies, my, my grass stalk? No," said Slimy, wiping his eyes with sad dignity. "No, I'll stay right here."

"And you?" asked the geese, their attention riveted on Noodle.

"Sorry, chaps, I think not. I'll stay with Slimy and take it like a string."

"Well," puffed the geese, flapping their wings, "we must be off! Good-bye and good luck!" And off they flew, rejoining their companions in a V-formation against the sky.

Slimy watched them fly away and looked at his own frail, skinny arms. "Why weren't we given wings to fly with?" he asked sadly. "It just doesn't seem fair."

"Fair! Oh, fair!" said Noodle, swinging on a sprig of cow vetch. "It just IS, my friend. As such, we must accept it." He nestled closely in a clump of dried weeds, huddling to keep warm.

"No," said Slimy, "I won't give up. There must be something I can do."

"Afraid not, old chap-o," chattered Noodle. "However, if you do come up with something, put me on to it, would you? Jack's coming soon; I can feel it. We've not much time left, my friend."

That night, Slimy huddled at the top of his grass stalk, gazing at the night sky—so black, with stars scattered like points of diamonds and the dust of jewels, so endless, so alive. *There must be an answer*, Slimy thought, as the biting wind whistled and moaned. *There must be a way.*

For days afterward, throngs of strings passed by Slimy's grass stalk, all trying to find warmer shelter. Some of the strings carried others on their backs who were too weak to go any farther. Still others shivered in the grass and dried leaves until they could shiver no more and were still.

One morning, Slimy awoke to see the world painted in crystals of white. Oh, it was wondrous, so beautiful, so cold!

Slimy tried to move, but had to lie quietly until the morning sun rose in the sky, melting the crystals on his eyes into shimmering rainbow pools of color. As the morning grew warmer, he called to his friend, Noodle, but only the wind whistled in return.

Slimy inched down off his stalk and checked the clump of dried weeds where his friend lay, huddled and quiet.

Slimy held his friend in his arms.

"It was Jack's doing, chap-o. He finally came last night. Paints the world in white, and that's the last sight a string gets to see. Good-bye old chap, and don't give up. Maybe you'll find a better way."

Tears filled Slimy's eyes as Noodle lay silently in his arms. "Is this what it means to die?" he wondered. "Good-bye, Noodle, my true friend. Maybe we'll meet again someday."

And he covered Noodle's motionless body with leaves and straw, said a prayer for his dear departed friend, and started on his way.

He thought at first that he would visit the home of a family of strings who lived under the roots of a spruce tree nearby. Perhaps they had found a way and would share their story with him. But, alas! When he reached his destination, all he found were rocks, dried-up leaves, and a bed of frozen moss where there once were living strings.

All through the day and night Slimy wandered, his exact path unknown to him. He only knew there was a way; there must be some way to make things different, to change the course of his destiny and, in so doing, to light the way for his fellow strings.

That night, Jack came again, this time with a coating of crystals so hard and white that tiny icicles began forming in the brooks and on the leaves of trees.

Slimy could take it no more. Weary and exhausted from the cold, he dragged his freezing body into a patch of warm darkness. Inside, he felt the heat of an unknown source. He huddled closer for warmth and soon was sound asleep.

That night, he had a dream. A beautiful fairy appeared to him in a blaze of shimmering white light, saying:

"I am the fairy of magical changes. Blessings to you, O Creature who believed so in a better way. Blessings on your pure and simple heart that rejoiced in the beauty of a simple day. For your perseverance through the odds, for the pure love in your heart for your fellow strings, you have changed your destiny. You have become more than just a string. You have become—a—woolly bear!

"From this moment on, you will have a coat that will always keep you warm, and, when winter comes, you will find a gift inside you that will transform you in the spring. This gift I give to you, so that because of you, all others of your nature may have it as well. From this moment on, I christen you — — Woolly Bear!"

In a halo of golden light, the fairy waved her magic wand, flashing stars and rainbows as she shimmered and suddenly disappeared.

Slimy opened his eyes and looked around him. What a wonderful dream he'd had. Next to him, sleeping peacefully, was a family of black bears. In fact, he was nestled in the warm black fur of one of the sleeping cubs, close by a sputtering, cheery campfire. Beside the fire, Mama Bear was busy at her sewing machine.

"La de da, la de dee, I'm as happy as a bear can be," she sang as she worked. Then she got up and trundled over to where Slimy lay, amazingly warm and peaceful by the fire. "Ah, you're awake, are you? Well, how does that suit fit you—all right? You were a bit of a frozen twig when you got here last night, frozen onto the leg of my youngest. I gathered some bits of fur from the floor of the cave, some black, some singed orange from the fire, and I made a coat for you! Poor devil, so skinny and cold, I had to do something to help." She held up some tiny coats in her big paw. "I made a few others too, just in case we find anymore of you out there."

Slimy sat up. He looked at his body. He patted his, well, he patted his fur from head to toe. No longer was he skinny and hairless! He was black—and orange and colorful and cozy and furry and, best of all—warm as toast!

Slimy threw his arms around Mama Bear, thanking her with all his heart. "I'm not Slimy anymore," he cried. "I'm Woolly!"

Then he remembered his dream. The fairy had said he had a secret gift inside of him.

Slimy, I mean, sorry, folks, Woolly climbed to the roof of the cave, and then something magical happened. A magical thread came out of Woolly's tail and began spinning a golden cocoon around him. Obviously, he'd never be cold again!

The thread wound its magical yarn until Woolly was enclosed in a gauzy casing of pearly fluff. It was so safe, so warm inside, that Woolly felt quite exhausted. He felt that he had learned all he could from his life as a string, and now all he wanted to do was rest. Memories of his life on the grass stalk, of his friends, the wind, the trees and the flowers, and of his dear companion, Noodle, flashed before his slumber-filled eyes. He yawned twice before falling fast asleep.

The winter snow flew frosty and white outside the warm cave where Woolly's cocoon lay perfectly still, held fast by magical threads to the ceiling.

The winter dragged on, until suddenly, from out of nowhere, a warm wind gushed its way north, melting the snow, and setting the healing sap to flowing through the trees.

Soon emerald green could be seen in spots in the woods and on the hills. Pale green leaves burst forth from winter's buds. The birds returned to grace the heavens once again. Spring had come.

Inside the cave, Mama and her cubs blinked open their sleepy eyes. All at once, they stopped to stare, as the once motionless cocoon began to shudder on the roof of the cave. A tiny hole was worked through the gauzy fluff, and then a strange new creature emerged.

The woolly bear felt something wondrous unfolding at his sides. With patient feelers, he worked at the sticky glue until he could feel the force of a wonderful power uplift him. Up, up he flew, out the entrance of the cave, and out, out into the marvelous sunlight!

The amazing flying creature thought to himself how lucky he was, how fortunate to be born into a world where his most fantastic dreams could come true! He must fly, fly among the creatures he knew and loved so well, and spread his message.

Woolly drifted in the warm currents of air until he spotted a caterpillar perched on the top of a dried-out stalk of timothy. He was orange and black and seemed familiar. Woolly flew down to chat with the striped caterpillar.

"Oh, hello, old chap. So it's you, is it? Seems I remember you, but I can't say from where."

Woolly's wings trembled in fond response. He, too, remembered this beautiful fellow, but he could not say where or when they had met.

"Yes, old chap, it's true. We've all got these coats to keep us warm now. What's your name, old chap? Mine's Bear. Woolly Bear. What's that? You're a woolly bear too? Well, I find that simply amazing, chap-o. How'd you get to look like that? Oh, sure, I'd love to fly, but I'm stuck here on the ground. What? Well, you don't say. Honestly, you remind me of an old friend I used to have, way back when. He thought there was a better way, too. Funny, I can't remember too well. . . ."

The two creatures sat on the top of the grass stalk in the warm spring air, sharing secrets and telling stories of strange and marvelous wonders, until one of them, realizing he could, spread his golden wings and suddenly floated up, up, up among the birds and buzzing insects, up, over the treetops, and away into the clear blue sky.

For Further Reading

ANONYMOUS, *A Course in Miracles*. Tiburon, CA: Foundation for Inner Peace, 1975.

ADAMSON, S., *Through the Gateway of the Heart: Account of Experience with MDMA and Other Empathogenic Substances*. San Francisco, CA: Four Trees Publications, 1985.

ASISTENT, N., *Why I Survive AIDS*. Fireside, 1991.

BORYSENKO, J., *Guilt is the Teacher, Love is the Lesson*. New York: Warner Books, 1990.

BRADSHAW, J., *Healing the Shame that Binds You*. Deerfield Beach, FL: Health Communications, Inc., 1988.

BURNETT, F., *The Secret Garden*. New York: Tor Books, 1991.

CAMPBELL, J. interviewed by Bill Moyers, *Joseph Campbell with Bill Moyers: The Power of Myth*. New York: Doubleday, 1988.

CAREY, K., *Return of the Bird Tribes*. New York: HarperCollins, 1991.

CASTANEDA, C., *Journey to Ixtlan: The Lessons of Don Juan*. New York: Pocket Books, 1972.

CASTANEDA, C., *Tales of Power*. New York: Pocket Books, 1974.

ESTES, C. P., "The Ugly Duckling" taken from *Women who Run with the Wolves*. New York: Ballantine Books, 1992.

GIBRAN, K., *The Prophet*. New York: Random House, 1923.

HALPERN, H. M., *How to Break Your Addiction to a Person: When and Why Love Doesn't Work and What to Do About It*. New York: MJF Books, 1982.

HAY, L. L., *You Can Heal Your Life*. Santa Monica, CA: Hay House, Inc., 1984.

HESSE, H., *Siddhartha*. New York: Bantam Books, 1983.

JUNG, C., *Man and His Symbols*. New York: Dell, 1968.

KRISHNAMURTI, J., *Think of These Things*. New York: Harper & Row, 1964.

KRISHNAMURTI, J., *Flight of the Eagle*. New York: Harper & Row, 1971.

KRISHNAMURTI, J., *The Awakening of Intelligence*. New York: Harper & Row, 1973.

KRISHNAMURTI, J., *Flame of Attention*. New York: Harper & Row, 1983.

MONROE, R. *Journeys Out of the Body*. New York: Doubleday, 1971.

MORSE, M., *Transformed by the Light*. New York: Villard Books, 1992.

PRABHAVANANDA, SWAMI & MANCHESTER, F., *The Upanishads: Breath of the Eternal*. Hollywood, CA: Vedanta Press, 1978.

SIEGEL, B. S., *Love, Medicine & Miracles*. New York: Harper & Row, 1986.

SIEGEL, B. S., *Peace, Love & Healing: Bodymind Communication and the Path to Self-Realization Exploration*. New York: Harper & Row, 1989.

SIEGEL, B. S., *How to Live Between Office Visits*. New York: Harper-Collins, 1993.

SIMONTON, O. C., *The Role of Belief in Cancer Therapy*. Pacific Palisades, CA: Simonton Cancer Center.

SIMONTON, O. C., *The Simonton Method*. Tape Nos. 400, 401, 402, 403. Pacific Palisades, CA: Simonton Cancer Center.

THOREAU, H. D., *Walden*. New York: Random House, 1991.

THURSTON, M., *Edgar Cayce's Dreams: Tonight's Answers for Tomorrow's Questions*. San Francisco, CA: Harper & Row, 1988.

TWEEDIE, I., *Daughter of Fire: A Diary of a Spiritual Training with a Sufi Master*. Nevada City, CA: Blue Dolphin Publishing, 1986.

WORDSWORTH, W., "I Wandered Lonely as a Cloud." London: Oxford University Press, 1923.

YOGANANDA, P., *Autobiography of a Yogi: The Divine Romance*. Los Angeles, Self-Realization Fellowship, 1974.

About the Author

ANGELA PASSIDOMO TRAFFORD was born in New York and spent her childhood on Long Island. She attended Adelphi University, majoring in Psychology. Angela worked as a therapist in various psychiatric hospitals including Mercy Hospital and South Nassau Hospital, on Long Island, and Guam Memorial, on Guam. It was then she began to realize that the bond of love and trust between therapist and patient seemed to be of truer significance for healing than any particular analytical school of thought.

After moving to the Canadian woods and having three children, Angela initiated extensive work on her inner self. She experienced many psychic phenomena and explored an arduous journey of self-realization. It was also during this time that she discovered what she now calls the "gift of cancer," which was soon to become a pathway to the transformation of her life.

Angela went through a series of chemotherapy and radiation treatments, but two years later, after moving to Naples, Florida, she had a recurrence of cancer. It was then, after prayer, that she discovered, Dr. Bernie Siegel's book, *Love, Medicine and Miracles*. She deeply identified with the personal philosophy of Dr. Siegel, and began to practice the visualization techniques outlined in his book. An account of the subsequent self-healing through the powerful light of love and energy is recounted in Dr. Siegel's book, *Peace, Love and Healing*.

As a result of this extraordinary experience, Angela felt a responsibility to share her message of hope with the seriously ill. She volunteered her services to the Naples Community Hospital, began a cancer support group, and founded her own practice, Self-Healing, in Naples, where she lives with her three children.

Recently Angela Trafford was the focus of a one-hour documentary special about healing on PBS. "The Heroic Path," a movie based on Angela's life and work, is in progress.

Workshops
with Angela Trafford

Angela creates a group experience of healing by sharing her own healing journey of self-realization, and using guided imagery and group meditation to facilitate the healing process.

Participants learn from Angela's own experience of healing herself of cancer and her work with cancer patients and others who are struggling to transform their health and their lives. The underlying message throughout is that of hope and joy.

Virtually everyone who has attended Angela's workshops finds them inspirational, enlightening and life-enhancing.

Illustration by Robert Lee

WORKSHOPS TOPICS

- Finding the authentic self
- Healing relationships
- Healing the inner child
- Spiritual transformation through the power of love and belief
- Creative visualization
- Healing through inner peace
- Reaching the creative intelligence through meditation
- Forgiveness
- Cancer and the healing of serious illness
- The power of love in healing

All meditations and visualizations included in this book are available on cassette tapes. To contact Angela or order additional Self-Healing tapes, call or write Self-Healing, 201 8th St. South, Suite 302A, Naples, FL 33940. (813) 434-6647.

Tapes may also be ordered from Varied Directions International, 69 Elm St., Camden, Maine 04843. (207) 236-8506.